The cat
that came in
from the cold

Waiting to come in from the cold

The cat
that came in
from the cold

The true story of a cat that learned
to obey commands

PHILIP BROWN

Photographs by the author

CHARLES SCRIBNER'S SONS
New York

By the same author

UNCLE WHISKERS

Printed in Great Britain
Library of Congress Catolog Card No. 78-59751

ISBN 0-684-15909-0

The cat
that came in
from the cold

I

My old marmalade hero, Uncle Whiskers, had died in October 1973. This left me without a personal interest in any living cat. I spent much of my spare time during the next twelve months writing the remarkable life that Uncle Whiskers had enjoyed – a long and active one in which he had triumphed over a near-fatal disaster that had overtaken him when he was only a year old and which had effectively deprived him of his two front legs.

Uncle Whiskers was a unique cat. I should never see the like of him again. This did not disturb me, because I had never really got deeply involved with any cat until Uncle Whiskers came on the scene and I had no intention of doing so again.

It was not until I settled to the task of writing his biography that I really appreciated what a remarkable cat Uncle Whiskers had been. It was not just his exceptional fortitude in the face of adversity nor his many engaging traits which struck me so forcibly in retrospect. It was the intelligence of the animal that seemed to me to be so extraordinary. I had known enough cats in my time to realise that some were much quicker in the uptake than others, but it was not until we had been thrown together in a sort of partnership after Uncle Whiskers' accident that I came to realise that a cat was not only capable of learning but could also, through trial and error, solve a few problems for itself.

The idea kept recurring in my mind that, given a really intelligent cat, one might well be able to teach it a great deal. Uncle Whiskers had mastered two words of command. A sharp 'No!' had always stopped him in his tracks, whilst he would leave the pantry or any other forbidden territory on being ordered 'Out!'. Both these commands involved negative actions and I now regretted that I had never attempted to carry his formal education any further.

By the time I was finishing the book in the autumn of 1973 I had it firmly in my mind that, given the opportunity, I should enjoy putting my theories into practice. At that time I still had five years to run to my retirement. Until then I would be in no position even to consider keeping a cat. The magnitude of the somewhat nebulous task that I wished to undertake did not, therefore, unduly worry me. I had five years to think about it and, even then, there would be the job of finding a young cat with a potential intelligence way above the average.

Of course my theoretical puss would have to learn the negative commands of 'No!' and 'Out!'. They are basic training if one wishes to live in harmony with any cat or dog about the house. I already knew that an intelligent cat would learn to obey them fairly quickly. But they would be kindergarten stuff for my imaginary feline prodigy. Cats have an irritating habit of occupying the most comfortable chairs. Would it be impossible to train one to do so only by invitation?

Any intelligent, well-trained house dog can be bidden to go to his basket. Why could not a cat do the same thing? A cat in the kitchen, especially when meals are being prepared, can be a nuisance. Puffing at my pipe, seeing my dream cat in the hazy blue smoke-rings, I saw myself saying 'basket' and at once the cat went to the basket and sat in it. If he was tempted to get out of it before I wished him to do so, I simply shouted 'No' and he stayed put.

Dog-owners who are conscientious enough regularly to exercise their charges much enjoy taking them on walks. Given a quiet, rural area, such as the one in which I hoped to live in my retirement, could not an intelligent cat be taken for a walk, as well as being allowed to rove about and hunt on its own? If a dog can be trained to walk to heel, why not a cat? It always seemed to be taken for granted that cats were too 'independent', too little influenced by their long association with humans, to be amenable to such useful disciplines, but was this true?

My dream cat was a Tom. In my admittedly limited experience I have found that Tom cats are usually more intelligent than Queans. If only to be a worthy successor to Uncle Whiskers, it would have to be a ginger. It would also have to be a youngster if it was to have a good chance of mastering its lessons. The chief difficulty, I felt, lay in finding a cat with a really high IQ. Whilst it is not difficult to spot dull-witted cats, it is impossible to ascertain whether a young cat is exceptionally well-endowed with intelligence until you have lived with it for at least several weeks. Having acquired a cat which you think might match up to your exacting requirements, it would be both unreasonable and unfair to have it put down simply because you have over-rated its mental abilities.

Putting theory into practice would be fraught with many hazards. I also knew from my experience of Uncle Whiskers that much time and patience would be involved. Perhaps by the time I was sixty-five I would feel I was too old to undertake the job – though I could, of course, use senility as a 'face-saver'. Those of my friends to whom I had confided my pipe-dream mostly considered I was already in my second childhood even to harbour such ridiculous notions. Cats were cats, they told me, and dogs were dogs. What cat would put up with the sort of silly nonsense I had in mind?

Perhaps the idea would become a reality, perhaps not. In the meantime my dream cat, a magnificently marked 'marmalader', would sit in its basket, looking first at an armchair and then at me. I pointed to a chair, said 'Hup! Hup!' and my visionary ginger immediately left his basket and jumped up into the chair, bursting into a purring song of delight.

Dream cats are wonderful creatures, affectionate, intelligent and obedient. Never any trouble and so inexpensive to keep! I came to love mine. The only drawback was that I could not show him off to an admiring circle of friends, none of whom had ever seen the like of him before.

II

Crossgill is a tiny village high up in the eastern fells of Cumbria. Enjoying hill-walking as I do, I was lucky enough to come across it quite by accident a good many years ago. It has one small but very good inn that offers not only excellent refreshment but modest accommodation. As Crossgill is not the real name of the village, which stands at the top of a dale almost completely sheltered by high fells, I will also give this pub a pseudonym and call it the Fox and Hounds. I have a small bedroom at the inn which is seldom occupied by anybody else. I also have the privilege of being entrusted, permanently, with a key.

When circumstances compelled me to part with Uncle Whiskers six years before his death in his fourteenth year, an old friend who then lived on the edge of the East Anglian fenlands and worked in Cambridge took him over. This kindly lady deals with all my literary work and is one of the few people who can read my scribbled long-hand. It was a stroke of good fortune that she also liked animals. When the cat was only ten years old she retired to Crossgill, being lucky enough to find a farmhouse perched high up the fellside in which to live. Here there was no through road-traffic of any kind and both her own ginger cat, Sammy, and Uncle Whiskers were able to roam at will. I would not be surprised if Uncle Whiskers regarded the last three years of his life as the best of them all.

Over many years I have made many good friends and acquaintances in Crossgill. It is a long way from the south of England but I go there whenever the opportunity occurs and I am never disappointed. It is always easy to relax in good company and it is splendid walking country, completely isolated from the main tourist routes and without any public transport whatsoever. The village itself, with its straggling, grey-stone houses and cottages and picturesque green dotted with the 'coronation' limes as its focal-point, may not be especially beautiful, but the setting amid the high fells is superb. Crossgill enjoys one of the lowest humidity rates in all Britain. In the summer it may be warm but is seldom hot. In winter it is often cold, crisp and gloriously sunny and frequently the whole landscape is covered in snow. The highest fells usually hold at least a little (and sometimes a lot) of snow from early November until late May. My impression is that either you don't like Crossgill at all or you lose your heart to it and its sturdy, friendly but highly independent natives. It is sheep-farming country, where folk work hard and play hard, with scant regard for the corridors of power in Whitehall. In many ways it leads the country on to better things: New Year's Day was a public holiday in Crossgill for years before it became an 'official' holiday in 1975.

Crossgill, for cats, can be either paradise or purgatory. Those cats that are properly looked after can consider themselves fortunate indeed. There is no traffic on the two roads that lead into the village, which is a 'dead end', and the risk of being run over by a car is extremely remote. There are plenty of voles, mice, rabbits and even a few rats to satisfy their hunting instincts. They can sit in the sun on the tops of the innumerable drystone walls and survey the landscape. For any cat that enjoys full board and lodging Crossgill is not far short of a feline nirvana.

Some of the farm cats, however, do not fare so well. Kept in order to cull the mice and rats around the farmhouses and outbuildings, they are apt to breed and multiply without check. Apart from milk, most of them have to hunt for their own food and, so long as they are not too thick on the ground, they probably do so successfully. However, the population on any given farm increases fairly quickly, so that the number of mouths soon outstrips the food supply, especially in winter, and the daily ration of milk has to be shared among too many. Then the stronger cats will probably drive the younger, weaker ones off the premises. The exiles have to fend for themselves, cadging a bit of charity at this cottage or that, raiding the dustbins at night and quenching their thirst with water from the burns. In summer and early autumn they manage to keep body and soul together. It is in winter and early spring that the crunch comes. A good many of these semi-feral cats probably go hungry in the winter months, especially if there is a spell of really bitter weather. Marauding foxes may spare some of the weakest ones from the final ordeal of slowly starving to death.

So long as Uncle Whiskers was alive I tried to get to the village about every month or six weeks, although in the summer the intervals were rather longer. Uncle Whiskers is buried in a friend's garden and I am happy to say that the daffodils that I planted on his grave have blossomed nobly every spring. His old ginger pal, Sammy, in his thirteenth year as I write, is still very much alive.

13

I enjoy Crossgill just as much in the winter months as I do in summer. Whilst I usually spend Christmas in the south, I always try to get up for the New Year and only once in the last ten years have I failed to do so. The days are very short at that season (by contrast, they are almost endless in June and July) and the evening sessions at the inn are always good fun. As with most rural hostelries, it is customary to serve breakfast at nine o'clock. This is vexing during the short days of winter, because by the time one has breakfasted a quarter of the short period of daylight has already passed. Since my friend migrated north with Uncle Whiskers and Sammy she has, bless her heart, almost always been prepared to give me breakfast as she is, by habit, an early riser. I walk up from the inn for the meal at eight o'clock in the morning. In mid-winter, should the sky be overcast, it is still almost dark at that hour.

I went up to Crossgill at the very end of 1974, to enjoy the New Year festivities. I had handed over the completed manuscript of my biography of Uncle Whiskers to my publishers, so I felt in a carefree mood. I had temporarily forgotten about my dream cat, reckoning I was all set for a week's good fun. After a long journey I arrived at the Fox and Hounds after nightfall. The evening of December 29 was frosty and clear and as there are no street lights worthy of mention within twenty miles, the sky was glittering with stars. The river was cascading over The Narrows and then chuckling away along its rocky bed under the bridge where, in a few months time, the dippers would be nesting amid all the buoyant bustle of yet another springtide. But although there was very little snow, it was deep winter now and all the trees lining the river – birches, alders, ashes, willows, sycamores and others – looked very dead in their stark, winter plumage.

In the bar of the inn there was, as usual, a cheerful log fire crackling away in the big hearth. It was like a homecoming and soon my old friends rolled in. We drank and yarned the evening away. I fell asleep as soon as I got into bed. I certainly did not dream about my dream cat. I did not dream at all.

The next morning dawned bright and clear. A warbling robin greeted me as soon as I let myself out of the inn and I had plenty of light to guide me as I strode up the rocky fellside, which was just as well, for there had been a heavy frost and the going was treacherous underfoot. I was ready for my breakfast and anxious to greet my old friend again. I went in through the wicket and up the three stone steps into the garden of her house. I paused for a moment to glance at the grave of Uncle Whiskers. It looked a little bleak and forlorn at this season, although the snowdrops were already pushing through, but my recollections of the old cat were warm enough. I could still clearly visualise him in my mind's eye, stumping along to greet me, tail stuck up in the air, purring with delight. As I walked briskly along the path that led round to the back of the house and the door into the kitchen, the thought crossed my mind that for so long as there was one person living who remembered Uncle Whiskers the cat would, in a way, remain immortal. But Uncle Whiskers had been dead for over a year.

Then came a surprise. As I turned the corner of the house and passed through another wicket into a small stone-flagged courtyard sheltered by a drystone wall, I caught a fleeting glimpse of a black and white cat as it darted round the farther end of the house, as if making

15

for the garage which is really an old cart shed with two big doors, and other outbuildings.

Over breakfast I received an explanation. My friend had seen this cat many times during the course of the previous five or six weeks. It was a very conspicuous cat, boldly marked. She considered it was one of the semi-feral strays, probably driven out of the village far below by its stronger, ruthless brethren. She had seen it sitting on or walking along the tops of drystone dykes. She had called to it but it would not come and when she had tried to approach the cat it had always bolted. It was obviously nervous, if not positively afraid of humans.

There had been a heavy snowfall towards the end of November. Traipsing out to get her coals early one morning she had seen the cat dart under the garage doors. When she let herself in it had disappeared. Two steps led down from the garage to her coal store which, incidentally, will take four or five tons with ease. Whilst getting the coals she had heard faint movements above the unsafe floor of a loft over the coal store. She tried to coax the cat down but it would not even show itself. In this bitter spell of weather it must have been living very rough, for the chill wind fairly whistled under the big stone tiles. That evening she had placed a saucerful of milk inside the garage. The next morning the saucer was empty. She had done this every night for some time. As the days passed she had seen more and more of the cat which, she said, had a very comical-looking face, with a dark spot above the right eye and another under the chin. It remained, however, almost as 'scary' as ever, bolting up into the loft whenever she tried to approach it.

She explained to me that she did not want another

16

cat in the house. Her ginger, Sam, had had the place to himself for over a year. He was over ten years old and she considered he would not, at his age, take kindly to a stranger. On the other hand, the pied cat was very thin and she would not let it starve. Because it always re-treated to the loft she suspected that it might have kittens, which would complicate things in due time. The kittens, she said, would have to be put down. When I suggested that the Quean might be put down at the same time she was quite indignant. The cat, I felt, was not without one good friend, anyway. But it certainly was not my dream cat. Whoever heard of a black and white cat marching obediently to its basket on the word of command? Anyway, if it was a female I felt that it was unlikely to have the sort of IQ that was necessary for my purposes.

If the romantic idea that I had suddenly stumbled across my dream cat had flashed momentarily across my mind, it did not linger. Nevertheless, I was warmed by the thought that the cat, by a stroke of good fortune, had landed up in a haven where she would never be allowed to starve. I was rather intrigued by the situation and, although it was really none of my business, I did not much care for the idea of the stranger roughing it in the bitter cold of the loft. Whether Sammy's nose was put out of joint or not, I reckoned it would be much more fun for all concerned if she came indoors. When I broached the idea, my friend was not over-enthusiastic. I suggested that, in the interests of her Sam, the door that led from the kitchen into the hall might be firmly closed, so that there would be no risk of any unexpected meeting between the two cats. We might then be able to lure the pied cat into the kitchen with a plateful of solid food. I was delighted when she

17

agreed to this suggestion, because it is always a challenge to try to gain the confidence of any half-wild cat or dog; if the operation is successful it is one of the most rewarding in the world. I knew that much from experience. I knew, also from experience, that it was a task which demanded limitless patience. I had time on my hands, for my next appointment was not until noon when I was due to meet some chums in the inn. I was excited by the whole prospect and fairly 'raring to go'.

A can of meat was quickly opened and a liberal portion scooped on to a plate. The fare had a strong, rather fishy smell, which suited my purpose admirably. My plan was simple. Whilst my friend remained tucked away in the corner of the kitchen I would quietly open the back door, tiptoe down to the garage, place the plate under that door and, full of hope, call the cat down from the loft. If I kept very still, it would see only the plate and my hand, which ought not to frighten it. If I could get it to start to eat in this way then, assuming it was as hungry as I had reason to believe it to be, I would be halfway to success. I would then gently pull the bowl outside the garage doors, remaining absolutely quiet. If the cat then came out and fed with me crouching beside her, all the rest, so I reckoned, would be easy. When she had eaten half the food I would back slowly towards the kitchen door, hoping she would follow. Once get her to feed inside the house, in the presence of two human beings, and victory was assured.

It was a splendid theory but I never got a chance to prove it in practice. On quietly opening the back door I came face to face with the cat, sitting on the stone flags about two yards away. I froze and for upwards of a minute we both stared at each other. I was anxious; the cat was suspicious. Very, very slowly I flexed my knees and lowered myself until I could hold the plate flat on the threshold of the door. Now the cat could see the meat. I think it also got a whiff of the fish. It stood up and then, slowly and warily, advanced. Equally slowly I backed away into the kitchen. The cat followed, crossed the threshold and came almost into the centre of the kitchen before it spotted the second occupant. Its nerve broke and it turned and went out of the door and out of sight. I could have wept with vexation.

However, it was obvious that the hungry cat needed the food very badly. It might not have gone far. It was important not to panic or do anything hastily. I put the plate down on the kitchen floor, almost plumb in the centre of the room and then moved over to the window alongside the open door, placing myself as far away from the door as possible. Nothing happened for at least two minutes. On occasions such as this, two minutes can seem an eternity. Then the cat suddenly ambled slowly through the door, looking warily to right and left before fixing its gaze on the food platter. It advanced very slowly, occasionally looking round over its shoulder as if fearful of an attack from the rear. But once it reached the plate it settled down and tucked in with rare gusto. On a signal my friend moved to the back door and quietly closed it. The cat scarcely looked up. When it had finished the solid food it spotted a saucerful of milk that had been put down for ginger Sam. It went over to it and proceeded to swallow the lot.

The cat had come in from the cold. It had not only come in but it showed no particular desire to go out again. It broke into a steady if not particularly loud purr, sat down and proceeded to wash its face. It *had* got a somewhat comical face, I had to admit. Although it was pitifully thin, it was thick-set, broad-chested and very big in the bone. In build it was more like some of the terrier breeds than a cat. Its coat lacked the silky sheen of a well-fed cat but it was remarkably clean considering the rough conditions in which the animal must have been living. I called the cat and it wandered over, brushing itself against my legs. I realised with relief that it was a Tom. My friend, who had been prepared to face all the complications of a whole brood of kittens, was relieved, too. She took up the empty plate and immediately the cat rushed over to her. He sat wide-eyed with anticipation as she spooned out the remainder of the contents of the can on to the plate. The moment she put it on the floor the cat wolfed it, then strolled over to the empty saucer. This was filled to the brim with creamy milk and was lapped up with gusto and a good deal of noise. When lapping, the newcomer reminded one of an elderly gentleman sucking his soup out of the spoon.

I suggested that now that he was inside it would be out of the question to throw the cat back into the cold. My friend agreed and the doorway into the hall was opened. With extraordinary confidence, the cat started to explore his new surroundings. He came suddenly face to face with ginger Sam, who spat, growled and then fled upstairs to an airing cupboard in the bathroom. Next the cat 'hoovered' the carpet under the dining-room table, apparently finding microscopic crumbs of bread or toast. Then he went to the hearthrug, stretched himself out, did a little half-hearted washing and fell asleep.

It was important to give him a name in order to get him accustomed as soon as possible to being called. My friend opted for Hoover, because of his treatment of the carpet. President Hoover would certainly be an impressive title but there were drawbacks. I pointed out that, when calling the cat up, a yell of 'hoov-hoov-hoov' would not carry far. So she suggested Timothy. It was not really relevant, but I pointed out that I had once had a cat called Timothy. So she settled for Uncle Timothy. She was going to look after the cat, not I, so I did not argue the point and Uncle Timothy it was.

The cat was sleeping so contentedly that it seemed impossible to believe that, less than an hour earlier, he had never entered the house. It was all very peaceful, with the sun flooding the fells and a crowd of tits and other birds feeding at the bird-table which was only a foot beyond the window. My good friend was justifiably proud of this bird-table, which attracted more than a dozen species in the course of the year. She had had a big pane of plate-glass put in, so that it was possible to watch the birds and see every detail of their plumage at a distance of only three or four feet. The birds were mostly very tame, at least as far as humans were concerned. Ginger Sam, fortunately, had always ignored them.

We did not know it but all this was the lull before the storm, and I was to bear the first brunt of that storm. The sudden arrival of Uncle Timothy had upset the cat catering programme. It was not just a question of feeding two cats instead of one, because Timothy was so under-nourished that for a time he would eat twice as much as any normal cat. So his landlady decided that she would drive into the nearest town and buy some liver and shin of beef. For an hour I should be left to guard the cat. I was instructed to ensure that Uncle Timothy, being a young Tom, did not slay Sam. I

21

accepted my responsibilities with an easy conscience. I knew that it was very unlikely that Timothy would attack Sam. I lit a pipe and settled down to watch the feeding birds.

I did not notice Uncle Timothy wake up. It was not until he jumped on to an armchair that I heard him move. My dream cat would never have jumped on to a chair unless he had been invited. But Uncle Timothy was not a ginger. Nor was he a dream cat, for the matter of that.

I turned back to watching the birds. Unfortunately I did not realise that I had a fellow-watcher until the cat slid off the chair on to the carpet, raced across the floor, leapt on to a small table just inside the window and banged his head against the plate-glass with enough force to knock out many a sturdy cat. He didn't appear to feel anything. All the birds had scattered in fright. The cat looked uncommonly pleased with himself.

If he was going to enjoy life with his landlady, this would not do. I picked him up by the scruff, said 'No! No! No!' and took him back to the armchair. He certainly was not frightened and he did not even appear to be properly deflated. I got myself a dining-room chair, placed it between the cat and the window and sat down. Now I watched the cat, not the birds. The latter very soon returned. Timothy's eyes widened. It was obvious that the temptation would prove irresistible.

The cat crouched and slid slowly forward to the edge of the armchair. I waited until he was about to glide on to the carpet before I bawled out 'No!' The effect was very gratifying. Timothy leapt back in the chair as if he had received an electric shock on the nose. Not wishing to be unnecessarily stern, I went over and stroked him, standing in front of him so that he could not see

22

the birds. There was obviously not a spark of malice in Uncle Timothy. He purred happily, rolling over on his back in the chair, so I returned to my own seat. In the next half-hour the cat made half a dozen attempts to reach the window. Mostly, I was able to stop him with a barked negative at the right moment, but once or twice I left it too late and he banged the window and all the birds, of course, flew off. I was surprised that he was picking up the lesson so fast. He was a topping cat but I still wondered whether, having roughed it for most of a shortish life, he would ever settle down as a house cat.

At the end of this half-hour of schooling he was tired enough to fall asleep. He slept on his back in a most unusual attitude, with all four paws stuck up in the air and unsupported. His chest and belly were pure white. Asleep in this posture, he looked almost angelic. And he was a big cat, too. Although the armchair was a full-sized one, he could not fit himself easily into it, so, when sleeping in this uncommon attitude, he had to turn his head at a right angle to his body. From the tip of his snout to the tip of his tail he was almost a yard of cat. He grew noticeably over the next few months and once he had got over the effects of semi-starvation he weighed just about fourteen pounds. Some cat!

Uncle Timothy was still sleeping when his landlady returned, yet not so deeply that he didn't wake up the moment he heard sounds in the kitchen. He tucked into a good meal of raw liver and lapped up another saucerful of milk. Whilst we enjoyed cups of coffee I told her about the cat's exploits with the birds. I said that I was confident that he could be cured of this habit but that he must never be allowed to get away with it.

She was vexed by this aspect of the cat's behaviour.

She made it very clear that she was not going to have her bird-pensioners driven off, especially during these short winter days when they had little enough daylight in which to stoke themselves up to withstand the long, bitter winter nights. I made a rash claim that before I departed at the end of the following week, I was sure that I could discipline the cat into abandoning this particular piece of misbehaviour. Even this failed to quell her wrath. If the birds were going to be frightened off time after time, even for a few days, she argued that most of them might never come back again. For the sake of his popularity-rating, I could only pray that Uncle Timothy would have enough intelligence to learn that 'No!' really meant 'No!'.

Due back in the Fox and Hounds at noon, I invited my friend to drink with me. If this sounds like a courteous gesture I am bound to admit that it did not spring from politeness. If we were both out of the house nobody would observe whether or not Uncle Timothy, on waking up, chased the birds away. It was decided that both cats had better be fed before we went down to the village. Ginger Sam, disturbed by the arrival of Uncle Timothy, had taken himself off somewhere upstairs in a fit of umbrage. However, as soon as they heard preparations going on in the kitchen, both cats arrived on the scene. Bearing in mind that he was asleep and also that he had only been in the house for three hours, I thought Timothy was pretty bright to be so quick off the mark. The notion that Uncle Timothy was likely to murder ginger Sam was soon exploded when the latter took a dab at the former, though no damage was done.

I was anxious to test Uncle Timothy's intelligence. I suggested that, when the plates of food were ready, I would take the cat and drop him out of the window beside the bird-table, just to see how quickly he could make the kitchen, which would involve him in going, one way or the other, right round the house. My friend protested that he might get lost (so she was worried about him, in spite of his attacks on her blessed birds!) but I pointed out that he must have been casing the joint for several weeks past.

The experiment involved dispersing the feeding birds but only for a moment. I held Uncle Timothy, not best pleased in being dragged away from the feasting, by the scruff and opened the window prior to depositing him on the ground below the bird-table. If he went to the right he would have to go all round the outbuildings to reach the back door but the only obstacle was a low stone wall. If he went left he would be taking the shorter route but he would have to round the angle of the house, swing out over the grass to clear a projecting summerhouse and then, at the last corner, either jump the wicket gate or a high stone wall before entering the finishing straight and dashing in to his meal through the open back door. He elected to go left, racing off without hesitation. I closed the window and marched towards the kitchen. In total distance he had to cover some thirty yards. He also had to make three right-angled turns and hurdle over the gate or the wall. He did it in about six seconds flat. By the time I had taken ten paces into the kitchen he was already guzzling. He was no fool, anyway!

Ginger Sam disappeared upstairs again. Uncle Timothy returned to the luxury of his armchair and was soon asleep, lying on his back with all four legs cocked up in the air. I placed another broad-backed armchair directly between the cat and the window in the hope that if he woke up but could not see the swarm of fluttering birds he would drop off again. Whether or not he chased the birds away in the absence of his benefactors will never be known. He was sleeping when we returned, the sun had dropped behind the south-western fells and the birds had all dispersed to their roosts.

The rest of the day was quiet enough. Sometime after dark Uncle Timothy went to the back door after demolishing his umpteenth meal and mewed softly. Although he always opened his mouth widely, his miaow was very quiet and gentlemanly. He was let out and quickly disappeared into the darkness. My friend was immediately concerned as to whether he would ever come back. I *knew* he would – and pretty quickly, too. It was suggested that the door be left open and the kitchen light left on. As it was already freezing outside this seemed to me to be an absurd notion. Besides that, I felt it was important to get the cat used to going in and out through the sittingroom window. For so long as the curtains were not drawn it would be easy to spot him immediately he leapt up on to the sill outside the window. Even if he was not noticed he would very soon draw attention to his presence. I won the argument; the back door was shut and we returned to the sitting-room. Within a minute or two Uncle Timothy appeared outside the plate-glass window. His black and white dress showed up to perfection against the outer darkness. He sat on each of our laps in turn, purring happily, and then settled on the hearthrug.

I do not think I was fully aware of the fact at the time, but Uncle Timothy was growing on me. It was hugely satisfying to have secured his complete trust within half a day. His behaviour that morning, when we had really had to bribe him with much-needed food to get him to come into the kitchen, had demonstrated that he had no good reason to put much faith in us, as just another lot of humans. Yet now he would not leave us. If either one of us left the room for any reason he would at once get up off the rug and follow close at heel, as if he feared that we might disappear from his ken forever.

I was anxious to see Uncle Timothy snugged down for the night before I returned to the inn early enough to enjoy a little liquid refreshment before retiring. The cat, without doubt, would have preferred to have stayed indoors, lolling in the unfamiliar comfort of a chair by the warm fire which was kept burning night and day. I even entered a plea on his behalf, although I was not surprised when it was rejected. For all his virtues, this cat was still a stranger in the house. He appeared to be scrupulously clean in his habits, despite his rough-and-ready background, yet there was no certainty that he would not blot his copybook overnight. An earth-box could be provided for him in the passage but he might not understand its purpose. The hide-out in the loft which he had probably occupied for weeks might have been uncomfortable and cold but he had been able to come and go as he pleased.

Anyway, the small summerhouse in which the cat was to spend the night was more than a mere cut above his old quarters. The wooden floorboards were carpeted and the curtains had been drawn across the windows to keep out the cold. A thick duffel-coat had been hanging all day above a radiator and this was to be spread over an old but comfortable armchair. If, from a feline point of view, the summerhouse was not exactly a four-star hotel, it certainly qualified for two.

Uncle Timothy was easily persuaded into his sleeping quarters by a platter of food and yet another saucerful of milk. With rather more faith than hope, an earthbox was placed on the floor. It was a frosty but very quiet night, without a zephyr of wind. The cat would be able to sleep for ten hours before his release on the following morning. He would come to no harm, anyway, and with the feeling that my duties towards him had been fulfilled, I set off for the inn, filling my lungs with gulps of that crisp, high-ground air which has a quality of champagne about it. Back at the inn, relaxing in front of a roaring log fire, I quaffed a pint or two of beer which induced a pleasant feeling of sleepiness. I had intended, once I got into bed, to do a little thinking about Uncle Timothy; but I was fast asleep within a minute or two of putting my head down.

The next day was New Year's Eve. In the far north of England, at any rate in rural areas, the New Year is welcomed in style. After midnight many folk keep open house and 'the footings' go on until dawn breaks somewhere between seven and eight o'clock. One can drop out, unnoticed, when one has had enough and only once, a good many years ago, have I summoned up sufficient stamina to see the revels through from start to finish. This unique experience was all the more remarkable because I had to travel down to London by train during New Year's Day!

It is traditional that a dark-haired man should be the first to cross the threshold after midnight, although how long after midnight does not matter. The 'first-footer' should have with him a small knob of coal, a little salt screwed up in a bit of paper for convenience, and a piece of bread. His first duty after entering the home is to put the coal on the fire to ensure warmth during the coming year. He then presents the salt to

28

the head of the household, so that all may enjoy good health, whilst the gift of the bread ensures that those who dwell in the house shall not lack sustenance.

Everybody who cares to do so troops in after the 'first-footer' to enjoy coffee, hot sausage rolls and other confections straight from the oven, or perhaps warm soup or hot curry, both of which are welcome fare for those who may have been tramping over crisp snow under a twinkling, starlit sky unadulterated by street-lights. There will, of course be a 'wee dram' to put new heart into the company as they set forth into the night for the next 'footing'. It is an old and simple tradition, as well as being immensely enjoyable although I must admit, in my declining years, that I have usually had enough by four o'clock on New Year's morning.

The prospect of the 'footing' alters the routine of most folk on New Year's Eve. The midday session in the Fox and Hounds is quieter than usual and in the evening few foregather in the bar much before ten o'clock. It is prudent to reserve one's strength for the 'footings', which may involve walking several miles. There is, after all, only one bridge over the river, although sturdy types have been known to cut their corners. A year or two ago one young man arrived at a 'footing' at three o'clock in the morning, wringing wet from the waist down. Although it was freezing hard he had plunged through the river on the darkest of nights. Wet or dry, clean or muddy – even if they have imbibed rather too freely and are 'gey fuzzed' – nobody can be refused entry to a 'footing'.

On that last day of 1974 I reckoned it should be a holiday in so far as Uncle Timothy's schooling was concerned. That is what I said to myself, anyway, when I climbed up the lane or loaning. The land was white with frost, the low sun already up and clothing the western fells with a tinge of pastel pink. The cat had survived his night in the summerhouse and had earned a commendation by using the earthbox, which showed intelligence. The moment the summerhouse door had been opened he had sprinted into the kitchen, to eat his breakfast.

He was still roaming round the kitchen, full of interest in all the novel things which were going on, apparently as eager as ever for more food and milk. When we both moved into the sitting-room Uncle Timothy followed us like a shadow. Then he blotted his copybook by scaring the birds away from the bird-table. Roaring 'No-no-no!', I took him by the scruff, putting him out into the hall and firmly closing the door. Within a minute the solid door shook loudly as Uncle Timothy gave it a mighty thump. The impact was so loud that I thought he might have hurt himself but as he proceeded to repeat the performance at intervals of a few seconds this seemed unlikely. The noise was considerable but most cats are sensible enough not to waste their energies indefinitely and as Uncle Timothy's impressive bangs were getting him nowhere I was confident he would soon desist. He did. The silence that ensued was a pleasant change and I smiled to myself at my knowingness. If he wanted to be a devil, I thought to myself, I'll soon show him who's the master!

Through the thick, wooden door we began to hear strange sounds in the hall – an irregular and not very loud *plock-plock*. Uncle Timothy could not be doing very much, but what was he doing? It was intriguing and our curiosity increased as the sound got louder. The hall was paved with stone flags, mostly covered by a fairly heavy length of carpeting about a yard in width and just over three in length. Although we racked our brains, we could not think of anything that he could damage.

After some minutes the sounds became intermittent with longer and longer intervals between the *plockings* and scufflings. This was not a case of curiosity killing the cat. It was one of curiosity getting the better of me. I just *had* to see what had happened. On opening the door I found that the cat had pulled up the hall carpeting into a loose, untidy mound. He was sitting on the top of it, looking as if he was mighty pleased with his handiwork. Then he caught a glimpse of the birds, made a dash through my legs and had scared them away with one of his much-favoured bangs against the window-pane.

My hostess was clearly very annoyed. My notion that there would be no schooling for the cat on this New Year's Eve went up in smoke. I took him from the table in front of the window and carried him by the scruff to the armchair, growling rebukes and showering him with negatives. He obviously wanted to be in that armchair. Far from being deflated, he started purring almost as soon as I had put him down. It is difficult to be vexed with a cat when it purrs but, aware of the fact that he had to be taught that this particular bit of behaviour was not to be tolerated, I remained stern and refused to stroke him or do anything that might give him the impression that I was anything but highly displeased with him. I took a chair and sat between the cat and the window, beyond which the hordes of hungry birds were already returning to their feasting. It was not long before Uncle Timothy was fascinated by them. He sat watching them, wide-eyed with growing excitement. As soon as he made a move I checked him with a rasping 'No!' He was learning fast and only once in the next twenty minutes or so, when my attention was momentarily distracted, did he make a break for it. After some more growling rebukes I got the impression that he realised at last that I was thoroughly annoyed with him. This was just what I wanted, for nothing brings home to a cat or dog the fact that it has mis-behaved more surely than the animal's awareness that what he has done has put him, temporarily, out of favour. It is more effective than hitting the creature and does not carry with it the very real risk of breaking the link of absolute trust which must be forged between the animal and yourself.

It was not long before Uncle Timothy, thwarted in his efforts to scare the birds away, indulged in a long spell of washing and then rolled himself over in the back of the armchair and fell asleep. It was a charming novelty to watch a cat which slept upside-down, all four legs stuck up in the air. I have known plenty of cats which, after sleeping curled-up, will stretch on awaking and then roll half-over so that they are temporarily on their backs but Uncle Timothy is the only one that sleeps soundly and for long periods in this attitude. Even now, having been familiar with this pose of his for some three years, it still makes me smile whenever I see it.

That night the New Year junketings went off in style. Uncle Timothy, once again shut up in the summerhouse, no doubt slept through them all. It was a lovely night, crisply cold, windless and without a cloud in the sky. A thick crescent of a moon was eclipsed by the western fells as the Old Year died but the stars twinkled on and the 'footers' traipsed to and fro as they have done for centuries past on every New

Year's morning. Yet Uncle Timothy, temporarily forgotten, managed to get into the picture before the night was over.

When his landlady returned from the 'footings' in the small hours she had not forgotten the cat. She had casually shone the torch on the summerhouse as she was about to pass it. One of the drawn curtains caught her eye because it seemed slightly disarranged and, dropping the beam of light, she looked into a round, black and white face with the familiar black smudges above the right eye and below the chin. The cat must have heard her passing through the wicket-gate, climbing the three stone steps and walking up the path. He had got on to the back of the armchair and then, putting his forelegs on the inner ledge of the window, had succeeded in pushing up a corner of the curtain. She spoke to the cat and was answered by a series of muffled miaows. The charmer was irresistible! She had entered the house, secured Sam in her own bedroom and then released Uncle Timothy from bondage. He had shot straight into the kitchen, apparently as ravenously hungry and as thirsty as ever. When she went upstairs to bed he had followed with the faithfulness of a shadow. She had not the heart to return him to the cold-storage of the summerhouse. So she put him in a spare bedroom; he settled down, purring with delight. She had shut him in and a few minutes later, dead weary, had tumbled into her own bed, leaving her door ajar so that Sam could roam around the house if he wished to do so. As she was dropping off to sleep she felt pleased that she had brought Uncle Timothy back into the house. She was in for a rude awakening.

In all fairness, not only had Uncle Timothy probably had enough sleep for one night but he found himself in strange surroundings. His landlady had scarcely dropped off before she was roused by a bang like a clap of thunder. Uncle Timothy, vexed by imprisonment, was practising his door-thumping trick. Thump, thump, THUMP! He could do no harm and she calculated he would soon weary of his efforts. Her calculations were correct. Uncle Timothy changed his tactics. At the very moment when she reckoned the worst was over, the *plocking* noises began. She smiled to herself. The carpet in the back or second, spare bedroom was an elderly one and the cat, surely, could not do much damage. Furthermore it was more or less firmly anchored by a bedstead, a divan and a chest-of-drawers.

The wretched brute got on with it. The noise increased. Unable to get to sleep she got out of bed to investigate. When she walked bare-footed out of her own bedroom door on to a small landing at the top of the stairs (a landing which gave access to all three bedrooms and the bathroom) she was surprised to find that she was treading on floorboards. A heavy runner, some six feet in length and half the width, had apparently vanished. She switched on the light and was able to confirm this astonishing fact.

She opened the door of the spare bedroom and Uncle Timothy bolted out like a rocket, racing downstairs to the kitchen. Switching on the bedroom light she discovered that the cat had managed to get his claws into the end of the landing runner which just intruded under the door. Inch by inch he had hauled the entire length of it into the bedroom. By the time she had replaced it the cat had come bounding up again and had leapt on to the bed, purring ecstatically.

What any cat could do once, she reasoned, it could easily do again. So she had shut the door of her own bedroom and, determined to get at least a bit of much-needed sleep, got into the bed in the spare room. Uncle Timothy got in beside her, purring with delight. She had turned her back on him but, after a minute or two, he climbed out on to the pillow, crossed to the other side and biffed his way under the sheets. She decided to give him best. Unlike the cat, she was very tired.

Just when she felt she was dozing off at last Uncle Timothy, probably because he was too hot, emerged from the bedclothes and settled down on top of her. Lean as he was from lack of food he was still a fair weight. She switched the light off and settled herself for sleep. The cat came up and sat on the pillow, still purring contentedly. Then he started licking her forehead – a pretty compliment, perhaps, but not appreciated in the circumstances. Preferring suffocation to this sort of provocation, she pulled the blankets up over her head.

By now, instead of being on the brink of dropping off, she found herself wide awake, listening for the next move of her tormentor. She had not long to wait. Uncle Timothy jumped off the bed and, as she had left the bedroom door ajar, ambled out on to the top landing and proceeded to savage the landing runner. She decided he could do little real harm to it and considered, optimistically, that the cat must soon exhaust his energy.

It seemed that he had begun to tire himself out. The noise of the runner-beating operation became intermittent. She had dozed off. She woke to one of the most terrifying of all sounds – the loud but somewhat muffled noise of a cat really attacking a carpet with the full force of its claws. Thus roused, she had gone into battle. The cat was savaging the carpeting on the half-landing where the broad stairway took a couple of right-angled turns to the hall below. As soon as she switched on the lights Uncle Timothy desisted and trotted downstairs to the kitchen.

Going downstairs herself, she had discovered that Uncle Timothy had also had a go at the hall runner, having pulled it up into a shapeless heap. Having restored the hall to some sort of order, she had gone into the kitchen where Uncle Timothy was prancing about as if it was his breakfast time. Apparently she had not securely closed her own bedroom door because ginger Sam, aroused from his own slumbers by the unusual uproar, suddenly ambled in to join the party. He, too, appeared to be thinking in terms of breakfast.

Anxious only to get at least an hour or two of peace and quiet, she decided that she might as well feed the brutes. So she went to the larder, followed eagerly by both cats. Now the late and much-lamented Uncle Whiskers and ginger Sam had at least learnt to obey the order of 'Out!'. If they entered the forbidden territory of the larder, this one word, uttered sharply, sent them packing. They left the larder, slowly and with dignity but without any argument. But the command, if given early enough, halted them from even crossing the larder threshold. On this memorable night when both cats followed her to the larder she had cried 'Out!' and, as she expected, Sam stopped in his tracks. It was unfortunate that, being very weary and therefore a bit slow in the uptake herself, she failed to appreciate that the word of command held no meaning for Uncle Timothy. It was also a bit of bad luck that, although this fact had not yet been discovered, Uncle Timothy's sense of smell was exceptionally acute, even for a cat. Whilst she was taking a jug of milk off a stone shelf she had her back to the larder door.

She heard a noise, followed by a low, throaty growl. She turned round just in time to see Uncle Timothy bolting out of the larder with a large piece of scalded liver which he had obviously pinched off a tin plate on the top of the 'fridge. She put down the jug and pursued the thief into the kitchen, where he had dived under a table, still growling over his booty. Determined not to give him a chance to consume his ill-gotten gains she got down on all fours and succeeded in dislodging him. It stands to the credit of the cat that he made no attempt to take a swipe at her bare hands with his forepaws. Instead he raced off with his plunder into the sitting-room, seeking refuge under a small bureau. By now the hunt was in full cry. The lady was determined not to allow the cat to have any chance of eating the liver. Uncle Timothy broke cover, dashed out of the room and ran upstairs. Somewhat breathlessly, she followed, but the cat had gone to ground under the spare room bed, from which it was difficult even to attempt to dislodge him. As the cat was already eating the liver, she decided to give him best. She consoled herself with the thought that it was what she would have given him for his breakfast, anyway. But the punch-line was still to come. She had left the larder door open and ginger Sam had seized the opportunity to scoff the rest of the liver at his leisure.

The two cats, both in deep disgrace but blissfully unaware of that fact, were asleep when I heard this tale of misadventure over a mid-morning cup of coffee on a bright and frosty New Year's Day. Almost unconsciously, I found myself stoutly defending Uncle Timothy. I pointed out that it was only forty-eight hours since he had first come in from the cold, that

37

during his life in the wild he had been able to come and go as he pleased and that he had been driven by sheer hunger to pinch anything that he could get his claws on, so long as it was edible. The lady pointed out that whilst I had been enjoying at least a few hours of sleep the wretched Uncle Timothy had prevented her from getting any real sleep at all. I took her point. Uncle Timothy would have to mend his ways if he was going to remain top of the feline pops.

Ginger Sam had never had any training as a youngster. For six years, however, he had shared the same billet with Uncle Whiskers. As Uncle Whiskers had learnt that the word 'Out' meant 'leave the room' (the room being most often the forbidden larder), Sam had soon picked up the lesson by example. During the next day or two I succeeded in making Uncle Timothy understand that on the command 'Out' he had best skiddaddle. After all, he had only to follow the example of Sam. When I went south early in January I had also managed to ram it into Uncle Timothy's noddle that 'No!' meant 'stop it', no matter what he was doing. In a week, therefore, I had taught him not to enter the larder and not to scare the birds away by leaping on to the table in front of the window. It was not much but it was a beginning, yet Uncle Timothy was still going to lead his landlady a merry dance before he began to appreciate that cats are not kings and that humans are not their subjects, ever at their beck and call, mere figures of convenience.

Whilst I sped southward by train I thought about Uncle Timothy. I knew I liked the cat. He had plenty of character and he had guts. If I had no evidence that he possessed a very high IQ, at least he was far from stupid. In learning to obey two words of command in a week he certainly showed promise, as they used to say in our old school reports. What I did not appreciate was that I was lucky in being able to withdraw from the front-line for three or four weeks. I missed Uncle Timothy rather more than he missed me.

III

On returning to the business and bustle of journalism I pushed Uncle Timothy into the back of my mind. In the evenings I sometimes had time to think about him. I was still fired with notions of turning him into a sort of super-cat who, in matters of obedience, would put many an ill-trained house-dog to shame. It is always fun to enjoy a few pipe-dreams.

After a few days I received a letter giving me some information about his background. Uncle Timothy had indeed begun his life on a farm, and had, as usual, been one of many. Nobody could actually recall him as a kitten – many of the cats on that farm were pied and in spite of his unusual and slightly comical facial markings he had never been particularly noted.

'Cats come and go, you know,' my friend had been told. 'We keep 'em for the rats and mice. They get a-plenty of milk. There are too many to know 'em all and they stray off, of course.' One could scarcely have expected more. If Uncle Timothy's origin had been traced with a fair degree of certainty, there was still no real clue to his age.

Some more news soon followed. The cat had been seen from time to time outside the front door of a small cottage in the village tenanted by a widow in her late seventies. In this case there was no doubt about his identity because several people had recognised his markings. An interview with the elderly widow revealed that she disliked cats. Oh! yes: she remembered the black and white 'thing'. It was as thin as a rake – not much more than a kitten. She couldn't stop it haunting her door, now could she? Her front door opened directly on the street. One night durin. the previous autumn, when the days were drawing in and the evenings coming on early, she had returned home after 'a wee bit chat' with a neighbour. It was too dark to see the dratted cat sitting beside her doorway or else, maybe, she just didn't notice it, which was the same thing really, wasn't it? Anyway, she had no sooner opened the door than the cat rushed in ahead of her. It was a fair bother and no mistake. It raked about the rooms and for some time she couldn't even find it. Dirty creatures, cats: mess anywhere, you know. Anyway, it had come down to the fireside and it was so thin she just had to give it a bit of milk. It had tried to settle down again in front of the warm fire but she wasn't having that. She had sent it packing. She should never have given it milk. The wretched creature hung about her door for weeks. Once or twice it had got in again and, stupid-like, she had given it more milk, which only made it stick around. She didn't want the thing. She didn't like cats and it was nothing to do with her, so she didn't give it any more milk. Sometimes it thumped on the door and she couldn't get any peace and quiet and whenever she went out in the dark she always had to remember the cat and shoo it away if it was hanging round. No, she hadn't seen the cat around for some weeks now – and didn't want to, neither. It was very thin, she remembered. She didn't think it would have survived the snowy spell before Christmas. It had probably died by now and that would be the best thing, really, because there were too many cats in

Crossgill, now weren't there?

Uncle Timothy, fortunately, was very much alive and building up his weight. It seemed unlikely that anything more would be discovered about his early days and what was known was vague enough. We could assume that he was not more than eighteen months old and certainly not less than nine. In the circumstances it seemed reasonable to regard him as about a year old when he had first come in from the cold on that morning of December 30, 1973. Anyway, that day is now regarded as Uncle Timothy's 'official' birthday.

IV

It was near the end of January and I was glad to be on the train heading for Crossgill. As I have said, I like Crossgill and the great areas of quiet, unspoilt fell and dale country surrounding the village, and it now had an additional attraction in Uncle Timothy. It is difficult to learn very much about the character of a cat on an acquaintanceship of not much more than a week. I knew that my plans for the schooling of Uncle Timothy, supposing they were not beyond the limits of even a highly intelligent cat's capabilities, would only succeed if I first took the trouble to understand the character of my pupil. If I could have had Uncle Timothy with me all the time I reckoned that I could have got to know him pretty well in a month or two, perhaps three at the most. But two months is, near enough, sixty days. On my journey north I pondered this problem, considering that it would be unlikely that in the whole course of the ensuing year I could be with the cat for as many as sixty days. If I could manage four weeks, all of which would have to be taken separately because of my work, I might tot up some thirty days. If I could add to that ten week-ends, I would still, at the year's end, be short of my target of sixty days – and those days, so I said to myself, would be necessary just to get to know how the cat ticked before I could tackle the task of teaching him a thing or two. Even then, I should only be in the company of the cat during the daytime and by no means throughout every precious day. Faced with the difference between theory and practice, my spirits dropped a little.

The next ten days would be great fun, anyway. I had liked the cat and I was thoroughly pleased with the prospect of meeting him again. I knew, for sure, that I would at least know and understand him better by the time I had to travel south once more. But I also knew that the ten days were not going to be as profitable as they might have been. An appointment had been made with the excellent local vet for Uncle Timothy to be doctored. Unless one has no sense of smell whatsoever, or a perverted one, an uncastrated fully mature Tom in the house is really intolerable, apart from the fact that the cat becomes a night-bird, keeping irregular and often highly inconvenient hours and sometimes disappearing for days on end. The appointment with the vet depended on the prevailing weather. To visit the vet involved a round journey of some fifty miles ('local' indeed!) over high fell roads up to 2,000 feet. Even a moderate snowfall with drifting renders the route impassable for traffic for anything from a day or two up to several weeks. One had to hope for the best.

During my absence of three weeks the relationship between the sitting tenant, ginger Sam, and the intruding Uncle Timothy had been remarkably good. Sam's nose had, of course, been put somewhat out of joint. He had periodically shown his umbrage by taking himself off upstairs and lying low in some hidy-hole, such as the airing cupboard. However, the two met periodically and always at meal-times. Whilst their food was being prepared it was always Sam who exhibited signs of aggression, mild as they were. If Uncle Timothy passed close to him he usually managed a swipe with an open-clawed paw *en passant*, even occasionally finishing up with a pawful of Uncle Timothy's fur. But Uncle Timothy's innate amiability was never shaken. He made no attempt to retaliate although, being much younger and bigger in build, he was certainly the stronger cat of the two.

Uncle Timothy's kindly landlady had, however, gone on labouring under the delusion that, until he had been doctored, Timothy might suddenly attack Sam and savage him severely. So long as she was up and about in the house she was confident that, should a real fight break out, she knew enough about cats to restore peace. But whenever she had gone out she had always shut Uncle Timothy in the back bedroom. He also slept in that room every night. Sometimes he had protested against this imprisonment by thumping the door several times, but he had learnt not to waste much energy when he was already tired so he had soon jumped up on the bed or a chair and fell asleep.

In the morning, I learnt, it had been a different story, most frustrating for Uncle Timothy. Ginger Sam usually woke up about six o'clock, when it was still pitch dark in midwinter, and demanded his breakfast. His mistress, fortunately an early-riser herself, would put on a dressing-gown and descend to the kitchen with Sam in close attendance. Uncle Timothy, hearing these preparations, knowing what was going on and feeling mighty hungry himself, went nearly mad. Apart from battering his prison door, he would haul in the heavy runner that stretched across the landing and proceed to beat it up to the best of his ability, which was pretty considerable.

When Sam had finished his breakfast he would go out into the darkness for his morning constitutional.

Then, at long last, Uncle Timothy would be released. I was told that he bolted out of the bedroom like a rocket, streaking downstairs with almost bewildering speed to attack his meal.

The weather was favourable and the long journey to the vet's surgery was uneventful. Uncle Timothy occasionally raised his voice from the depths of a capacious wicker basket but he was in no discomfort although this must surely have been the first occasion on which he had travelled by car. Four weeks of good and varied nourishment had transformed him. His coat now shone like silk and he had acquired the amount of flesh that his big-boned frame was intended to carry. I could see that this was so, and I also felt it when I had to carry him in the wicker basket from the carpark to the surgery – a distance not far short of half a mile and uphill most of the way. A stone always weighs fourteen pounds, I know, but I can say that it seems much heavier when carried in a large and rather awkwardly shaped basket, especially when the lively inmate perpetually shuffles round, thus upsetting the balance of the whole thing.

When collected an hour or two later Uncle Timothy was still under the influence of the anaesthetic. He remained quiet throughout the return journey and when I eventually transferred him from the wicker basket to the comfort of the best armchair, he hardly opened an eyelid. It was not until teatime that he lurched out of his comatose state, sitting up unsteadily in the chair, his head rolling about as if he were tipsy. He suddenly decided to transfer himself to another chair about six feet away. He half-jumped, half-fell to the floor, almost tumbling head-over-heels on landing. He staggered over the few feet, tried to steady himself and then took

On business bent

Waiting is a bore, especially when you're hungry

. . . action at last . . .

. . . they say I'm big but . . .

. . . I can squeeze through a five-inch gap

*Life is easier if you
don't argue . . .*

*. . . and if I'm told
to sit on my cushion . . .*

. . . I'll sit on my cushion. It pleases the master but . . .

. . . it's useless for sleeping on

*I **must** be good – I've been given a big dog-basket*

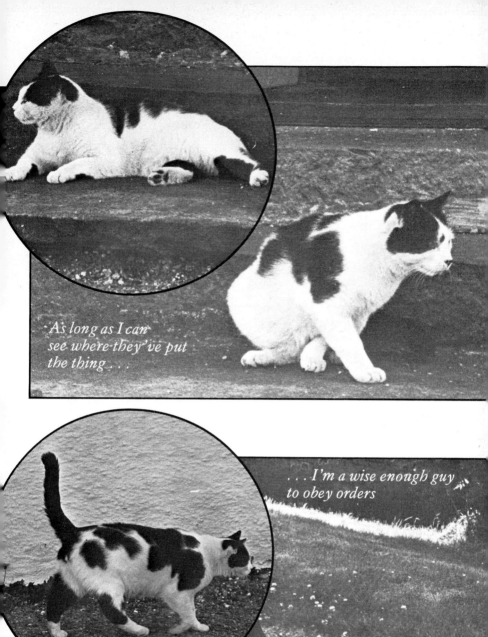

*As long as I can
see where they've put
the thing . . .*

*. . . I'm a wise enough guy
to obey orders*

If you really want a walk . . .

. . . let's go

*. . . I know all the
short cuts . . .*

*. . . and never jump a wall
here is a stile . . .

. . . I wonder what's down there? . . .

. . . Almost home!

The watchers: Uncle Timothy and Ginger Sam

Late for dinner?

If you're going to take my photo . . .   *. . . I had better wash my face*

Please don't disturb

a shaky sort of leap which, more by luck than judg-
ment, landed him on the seat of the chair. He toppled
over and fell asleep. The new chair did not look any
more comfortable than the one he had been using and I
wondered what prompted him to swop seats in his be-
fuddled state. Anyway, the cat was almost back to
normal when I left for the inn in the evening.

Uncle Timothy no longer had to be closeted in the
back bedroom. The door was left ajar and usually, towards the end of the night, he moved into his landlady's
room where he leapt up on to her bed. This manoeuvre
usually woke her up, the cat received a few kind words
and, purring ecstatically, moved off to a chair. Freed
from the frustrations of solitary confinement, Uncle
Timothy abandoned his vexatious habit of drawing
attention to himself and working off his aggravation by
thumping on doors, piling up rugs or even tearing up
carpets. He was, in fact, a pretty good cat about the
house. He never once used his claws on wallpaper or
upholstery. Although it was only a few weeks since he
had lived in a house, he fell into the routine in a
remarkable way. Except in the foulest weather he used
to go out after breakfast, making his exit either through
the back door from the kitchen or by way of the sitting-
room window. Daylight or dark, he almost invariably
re-entered his home via the sitting-room window. After
nightfall, if Uncle Timothy was out, the curtains of this
room were always left undrawn so that the cat, with his
bold black and white markings, could be spotted as
soon as he leapt up on to the outer sill. If the room was
temporarily unoccupied he would wait patiently, but if
there was somebody there and his arrival had not been
noted he would give a series of miaows. In the rare
event of these not being heard, he would thump the

49

plate-glass pane.

Uncle Timothy's voice was one of some compass. Considering that he is a really big cat, his mew is quiet enough. He uses it mostly as a greeting. Out of doors, if he is called by somebody he knows or if he recognises a friend without being called, he will come to them with black tail raised vertically and when he reaches them he will miaow several times before breaking into a purr. Even today he remains extremely wary of strangers, but once a visitor has been allowed into the house the cat is completely at ease. If Uncle Timothy's mews are comparatively soft, his growls are quite the reverse. He is easily the best feline growler I have ever known.

This story would become tedious if every incident had to be dealt with in chronological order. On the subject of Uncle Timothy's vocal powers I will therefore release myself, albeit temporarily, from the strait-jacket of time. Uncle Timothy's home is surrounded by fields divided by high stone dykes. Some of these pastures are earmarked in late spring for mowing-meadows but otherwise they are grazed, mainly by sheep but also by a few cattle, more especially young bullocks and heifers in the warmer months. Most of the pastures remain reasonably damp even in dry weather so that there is plenty of 'bite' for the feeding stock.

Uncle Timothy got along well with the sheep and lambs. In spite of their greater size, he roamed through them on his rabbiting forays without let or hindrance. He ignored sheep and they ignored him. Young cattle were different. They were curious and as he sat waiting and watching for rabbits they would slowly approach him *en masse*. Uncle Timothy did not welcome their advances. They spoilt his sport, for one thing. He

50

would turn to sit facing them and then growl at them continuously. Sometimes the cattle would remain at what he considered a respectful distance. More often than not they would come closer and closer until he considered that discretion was the better part of valour. He would then walk, not run, to the nearest drystone wall and jump on the top of it, perhaps using a convenient keystone or *through* (pronounced 'thruff') to make the leap the easier way by taking it in two halves. Once on the wall-top, he was as high or higher than the cattle. He was probably also well aware that in an emergency he could drop down to safety on the far side of the wall. Anyway, he would turn to face the beasts and at the same time break out into his loud and continuous grumbling, throaty growls. As often as not the cattle, still fascinated, would move forward and gather round him in a rough semi-circle. The whole performance then looked uncommonly like an open-air concert, with the *basso-profundo* singing away to a rapt and silent audience.

I must, if reluctantly, tell a story against myself. One quiet winter's evening when I was staying in Crossgill I was dining with Uncle Timothy's landlady. During the meal Uncle Timothy was fast asleep in an armchair within three feet of me. Possibly I had imbibed too much gassy beer at the Fox and Hounds or maybe I was overeating myself. Be that as it may, towards the end of the feast my tummy suddenly started rumbling. Uncle Timothy woke up, glared wide-eyed under the table and started to growl loudly. Fortunately my internal rumblings only lasted a few seconds. But the cat was not satisfied. Still grumbling throatily he jumped down and searched round the room, only returning to his chair when he was absolutely satisfied that no strange

51

creature had had the temerity to invade the very heart of his territory.

Returning to that week at the end of January, 1974, once Uncle Timothy had been doctored it was obvious that life was going to be much easier, both for him and his guardian. It was understandable that the cat, having lived a life in which he could come and go as he pleased, had been frustrated by the restrictions placed upon him to prevent him murdering Sam. Once these irksome restrictions were lifted he gave up carpet-bashing and thumping doors. He had cottoned on to the fact that the larder was taboo. He no longer had a chance to thieve. But when his meals were being prepared he would often sit on a stool beside the table, purring in anticipation. Occasionally he would rise and put his paws on the edge of the table with the obvious intention of having a grab at a morsel. A sharp 'No'! was enough to make him sit back on his haunches. He had, in fact, learnt the proper response to the negative command in the space of four weeks, which was not bad going. I had feared that a cat which had lived wild for the only year of its life would present problems when it seized the chance to live in a good boarding house, with all food found. It did not work out that way at all. Perhaps half a dozen times he made use of an earth-box which was always available in case of an emergency. He had, after all, been accustomed to being free to get out of what rough shelter he had been able to find without let or hindrance, by day or by night. However, he soon slipped into the new rhythm of life.

If one is going to live amicably with a cat and if both parties are going to get the best out of the partnership, a good deal of patience and a certain amount of discipline is necessary on both sides. When a cat is out of doors it should be free to do as it pleases, which does not mean that it can stroll back just when it likes and that the whole routine of the home should be turned upside down simply to accommodate its selfish eccentricities. Looking back, I am aware that I may have made that mistake with Uncle Whiskers, but he was a sorely crippled creature. Special cases merit special treatment. Uncle Timothy was as physically fit as the best of cats.

When he first landed up in his only real home he was so delighted and apparently so anxious not to let his benefactors out of his sight for long, that he used to go in and out of the house all the day through. If he were absent for more than half an hour his devoted landlady, without any good reason whatsoever, feared that he might either have taken himself off to another home, got lost or been killed or maimed by some half-wild dog. This in-and-out behaviour of the cat was unlikely to continue indefinitely and from the outset it was laid down that he would not be permitted to go out after eight o'clock in the evening, although it was agreed that this should be extended to nine o'clock during that period of the year when British Summer Time was in force. Most cats, like many other animals, have a kind of inbuilt sense of time, but they cannot be expected to put their watches either on or back one hour, twice a year.

Uncle Timothy accepted this schedule in a manner which has never ceased to astonish me. Quite often, especially when it is still daylight (as it is in high summer at 9.0 p.m.) or on fine, moonlit winter nights, he comes home for his supper after the official closing-hour for 'outs' and, having enjoyed his meal, marches to the sitting-room window. Two or three sharp nega-

53

tives are enough to get the message over to him that he is not going out again that night. It is as simple as that.

Uncle Timothy's daily routine soon developed into a regular pattern which has been maintained over the years. He has his breakfast about six in the morning, except in winter when it is pitch dark at that hour, in which case he may sleep on for another hour, and in summer when the sun is up by five and he often likes to get out at that time. Except in very inclement weather he is usually out and about for several hours after his breakfast. After his midday meal – sometimes even for an hour or two before it, as well – he sleeps soundly, becoming active again around 4.0 p.m. or 5.0 p.m. and going out until supper is due at eight. Only if he is on time for supper is he allowed out after it. There is more than an even chance that he will be back home for the night before nine. If he is not back by then it is the custom to give him a call or two, both from the back and the front of the house. If the cat is within ear-shot he will appear at the sitting-room window within ten or fifteen minutes, if not sooner. He may, of course, be out of earshot but he seldom fails to return home later than ten o'clock. In two and a half years there have not been more than thirty or forty such incidents and only a handful when he has not landed back by eleven. Only once in all this time has Uncle Timothy spent a night out. It is an amusing episode, so that even if it is yet another story against myself it should be put on record.

It happened on the first week end of November, 1975, when Uncle Timothy was old enough to know better. I had booked in for a week at the Fox and Hounds but I had undertaken to stay in the house on the fell over the first week-end in order that Timothy's landlady could get a short break to visit relatives. My main task, of course, was to look after the two cats. I had strict instructions not to let Sam out once he had returned after dark.

I was delighted with this opportunity of having a week-end with Uncle Timothy. It was arranged that I should spend my three nights in the third, rarely used back bedroom, which was Uncle Timothy's normal sleeping-quarters. All went well on the first, Friday, evening. There was some rain after dusk and Sam showed no wish to go out. Uncle Timothy went out and in two or three times after nightfall but he did not care much for the rain, either, and snugged himself down quite early. Asleep on the bed, he awoke and purred delightedly when I appeared in the bedroom.

The following evening was fine and quiet. However, Sam hardly went out at all throughout the day. Timothy slept through the afternoon, went out at dusk and did not return until seven o'clock. He ate his supper and, obviously busy with some ploy, possibly rabbit-hunting, he went off again at once. Ginger Sam then decided he wished to go out, too. He got really worked up about it, roaming from the sitting-room window to the back door and back again, to and fro. Unlike Uncle Timothy, he had never learnt to obey the command 'No!', so he really made something of a nuisance of himself. I let off steam by calling him names of which his absent owner would certainly not have approved. He became so bothersome that it occurred to me that he might have urgent reasons for getting out but, in view of my instructions, I considered that if this was so he must make use of the emergency earth-box. Most cats loathe to use a box and I felt rather sorry for Sam. My sympathies were misplaced, because the big schemozzle turned out to be mere feline bluff. After a while he gave it up and disappeared upstairs. I reckoned he would sleep for the night.

As time rolled by I waited expectantly for Uncle Timothy to appear at the window. Sometime after nine o'clock I gave him a call. At ten o'clock he still had not come. I took a torch, went out and prowled round the house for five or ten minutes, bawling my head off. I knew that Uncle Timothy was well able to look after himself. If I went up to bed he could sleep snugly enough in the summerhouse, for it was not even a cold night. On the other hand, over nearly two years he had not once failed to return in the evening, even if once or twice it had been as late as midnight. I had taught the cat everything he had ever learnt. I had paid for his keep and his vet's bills from the outset. I considered him to be my cat, although the amount of time I was able to spend in his company was not great. I felt it would be rather disgraceful if I had to admit to his land-lady, when she returned, that he had failed to put in an appearance overnight.

With one eye I watched a boring TV programme, with the other I squinted at the window, anticipating his sudden, welcome appearance as he leapt up on to the outer sill. Sometime around eleven o'clock I decided to open the sitting-room window and give him another yell or two. I was tired, vexed and off my guard. I opened the window wide, pushed my head out into the darkness and bawled for Timothy. Suddenly I realised that Sam had leapt on to the table beside me and was just about to get airborne as he dived out into the night. To lose Uncle Timothy was one thing. To lose ginger Sam was another – a fate too awful to con-template. My own reflexes surprised me as I made a grab at the flying cat and just caught him by the stump of his tail. This would not have hurt him but he let out a yell of indignation as I tightened my grip whilst he dangled head down for a few seconds before I was in a position to haul him back into the room. Sam made it very clear to me that he did not think much of my behaviour but we made it up when I gave him an unexpected plateful of liver.

Meanwhile there was no sign of Uncle Timothy. At midnight I gave him another call and opened the summerhouse. A few minutes later I went up to bed. Temporarily I was fed up with the cat and all his works. Why should he choose this night of all nights, wretched little brute, to play up? I washed and got into bed, happy in the knowledge that he would turn up in the morning. And if he came to the window and could not get in, he would learn a salutary lesson.

I normally sleep for about six hours. However, in a strange bed I doubt if one sleeps as soundly as usual. Anyway, on this occasion something woke me up. What was it? I looked at my watch – ten minutes to two in the morning. I listened. Was that Uncle Timothy mewing? Imagination? I turned over and relaxed. Was that a thump on the door? Why worry, anyway? Uncle Timothy would be okay in the summerhouse. Then I thought to myself: if he is at the window or the door and I go down and let him in I shall at least be able to claim that the cat has come back every night. So down I went, pottering round the house with a torch in pyjamas and a dressing-gown. Uncle Timothy was not in the summerhouse nor did he come to a call. I went back to bed and slept until daybreak.

On waking I went down to the kitchen, out of the backdoor and into the summerhouse. It was disconcerting to find that Uncle Timothy was not there. He had been gone for more than twelve hours – an unprecedented happening – and for the first time I felt some anxiety. I turned back through the wicket-gate. Emerging from the garage at the other end of the house, moving very slowly and stretching himself after what must have been a sleep of at least several hours, was Uncle Timothy. It may have been unintentional, but he managed very successfully to convey to me the impression that he really could not fathom what all the brou-ha-ha was about. I was so relieved to see him that I refrained from telling the cat exactly what I thought of his behaviour. Even at that time his vocabulary was limited to about half a dozen words, so my vitriolic blasting would have been wasted, anyway.

Back in that January of 1974, when Uncle Timothy had only known for a month what it was like to enjoy food and shelter, the cat had only revealed a part of his remarkable character. Of the eight or nine days of my stay in Crossgill, two had flown by the time Uncle Timothy had recovered from his trip to the vet: it was not the operation but the anaesthetic that upset him. He was not sick, just dopey.

At the time I felt that I required much more experience with the cat before I took my training schemes any further. In the interests of peaceful co-existence, it had been essential to subject Uncle Timothy to a 'crammer' course about the interpretation he must be made to put on 'No!' and 'Out!'. But until I had had a chance to get to know him better, thus gaining some idea of his capabilities, it might be prudent to play a waiting game.

In the brief time at my disposal, therefore, I concentrated on two things. The first was positive. I took

58

several walks with the cat, usually following him fairly closely but not so closely that I had any marked influence on his own inclinations although, quite often when he looked round and espied me, he would come trotting back, tail held high, to greet me effusively. Uncle Timothy had become very much attached. He was no longer an independent cat and this, in my belief, is the first requirement if any close understanding is to be reached with a cat, and until that understanding is established any progress towards a good companionship between man and beast is unlikely. But in working towards a successful association of this kind it had better be appreciated that the man, as well as the cat, must be willing to sacrifice some of his independence, too.

During these early strolls with Uncle Timothy I learnt a lot. He obviously had a good nose, questing over the ground much more slowly but with all the thoroughness of a good hound. He was ever-curious, never by-passing anything that was worth a look and I soon discovered that almost anything deserved examination, from a ruined barn to any sort of hole. Rabbit burrows were especially favoured in this respect, although rabbits were scarce in mid-winter. In that limestone country underground springs were frequently paved over with large flat stones. Often, largely due to the passage of time, a part or the whole of one of the covering stones was missing. If there was a sizeable hole as a result, Uncle Timothy would be sure to shove his head in and peer down into the murky depths. If I said that in the course of a few strolls together Uncle Timothy convinced me that he had all the makings of a great hunting cat, I should be overlooking the fact that for many months he had had to hunt to live.

I have already mentioned my theory that it should be possible to teach an intelligent cat to walk to heel. On these first rambles with the cat I attempted, if only in a very tentative way, to translate theory into practice. If he were well ahead of me I would give him a call. He would usually stop and look round, sometimes sitting down as if waiting for me to catch up with him. I would stand my ground and call him again. Nine times out of ten, after two or three calls, he would come trotting back to me and I would give him a bit of a cossetting, whereupon he purred with pleasure. I would do much the same thing if he lagged behind. Occasionally, when he was on a path and well ahead of me, I could see that he was about to turn off through a gateway into a meadow. If I bawled out 'No!' he would pause and look back at me. If I repeated the injunction once or twice the cat would, more often than not, sit down and wait for me to catch up with him.

As an exercise in control I found all this mildly amusing but it was not particularly positive. Much more to the point was that I experienced great pleasure in being in the cat's company. He was very active, enterprising and intelligent. On all but the stormiest days he was out and about for more than twelve hours a day, as well as being alert and wakeful for a good deal of the time he spent in the house. He slept soundly for six or seven hours at night and usually for two or three during the day, but when the longer days arrived his sleeping-time did not exceed eight hours a day. It is frequently alleged that cats spend more than half their lives in sleep. Unfortunately many cats, by the very nature of their over-domesticated and restricted lives, are bored to death. Boredom is the natural sire of laziness and sleep. What else is there to do?

After five weeks of living in the unaccustomed luxury of a good home and enjoying regular meals, Uncle Timothy could rarely be faulted in his immediate and correct reaction to the command 'No!'. In a relatively short period of time he had been taught to resist the old temptation to rush to the window and drive the feeding tits, robins and finches off the bird-table.

Uncle Timothy had lost interest in birds although once he achieved a 'spectacular' in catching a cock chaffinch. Anxious to keep in close touch with the cat, I had managed to get up to Crossgill for a few days at the end of February 1974. One sunny afternoon I was watching a host of birds, all in their brilliant spring plumage, fighting for a place on the bird-table. The tits all cleared off for a while and a fine cock chaffinch had the table to himself and was making the most of it. Now a male chaffinch in his best plumage, watched through a clear sheet of plate-glass at a distance of only four or five feet on a day of brilliant sunshine, is a beautiful sight.

I was sitting in a low chair, so that I could only see the table itself above the lower lip of the window. The table, supported by a post driven firmly into the ground, was three feet above the path that ran below it. Unbeknown to me, Uncle Timothy must have been sitting on the path directly below the table and, now I come to think of it, his presence might have accounted for the temporary absence of all the tits. Whilst it was feeding on the table the chaffinch must have been invisible to Uncle Timothy, although the cat would have heard it pecking away at the crumbs.

Having feasted well, the chaffinch took off and simultaneously, and much to my astonishment, two black and white paws shot up above the far edge of the table

61

and paws and chaffinch disappeared downwards. Uncle Timothy killed the chaffinch but he clearly did not like the feel of feathers in his mouth and made no attempt to eat it. If I felt a little sorry for the chaffinch I had to take my hat off to the cat. He had had to leap up over three feet, which is no mean achievement for a big, heavy cat, whilst the speed and timing of his jump was extraordinary. The reward for his polished performance was totally inadequate.

My work kept me very busy in the summer months. Even my week-ends were seldom free. I set great store, after the late February visit, by a trip to Crossgill at Easter, for I knew that, apart from odd week-ends when my business took me up North, I would not again be with Uncle Timothy until the end of August.

Easter was late in 1974, falling in the middle of April. Good Friday and Saturday were rather miserable at Crossgill but the following three days were sunny and springlike. I tried taking Uncle Timothy for a few more walks. I think that he enjoyed the company, for he had quickly developed into one of the most companionable of cats, not only almost invariably coming when called but also whenever he spotted you if you were prowling around. Yet I became more and more aware of the fact that these walks were somewhat frustrating for the cat and unprofitable for myself. Unfortunately it took me some time to realise that the most enjoyable thing for both of us was to allow Uncle Timothy to take me for a walk instead of *vice-versa*.

So far as Uncle Timothy's education was concerned, only one thing was achieved that Easter-tide, yet it was important. Given the chance, the cat had a habit of getting on one of the two most comfortable chairs in the sitting-room. If the lady of the house was on her own this did not raise any complications but when, as she frequently did during the summer months, she had guests staying with her, things would be different. Cats can rest or sleep very comfortably on a rug on the floor. Humans, in my experience, cannot. One can, of course, turn a cat out of a chair if one wants it for oneself, but this is scarcely fair to the cat. I see no reason why a sleeping cat should be disturbed in this way if it can be avoided, so I set myself the job of putting things right.

The first part of the drill was simple. Uncle Timothy understood that 'No!' meant 'don't'. Whenever he made a move to get into a chair, therefore, he was stopped in his tracks with a sharp negative. The second, equally important, part was rather more difficult. It would be tedious in the extreme always to say 'No!' whenever the cat exhibited a desire to jump into a chair. Furthermore, if this drill was carried on indefinitely, the poor creature would soon conclude that he was never to be allowed to use a chair, which was certainly not my intention. What I wanted him to do was to use a chair by invitation. I realised that this could only be successfully achieved – if, indeed, it could be achieved at all – when somebody was present in the house. It would be too much to expect that, in the absence of his landlady perhaps for half a day or longer, the cat would refrain from making use of any chair that happened to take his fancy. It did not matter, anyway, if nobody was about.

I decided that 'Up! Up!' was sufficiently distinct from the two other words he already understood to serve my purpose. Having stopped him from moving off the hearthrug into a chair with a rapped-out 'No!' I let him lie for at least five or ten minutes. Then, provided that one of his two favoured armchairs was not occupied, I attracted his attention with a nice-toned but brisk 'Hup! Hup!'. It was not surprising, of course, that he looked at me with some bewilderment. After all, he had never heard me make this noise before. So I pointed at the chair, even patted it in invitation, and repeated my 'Hup! Hup!'. It was, at first, undoubtedly the pointing and the patting that did the trick, yet only a few repeats of the performance were necessary before he cottoned on to the fact that 'Hup! Hup!' gave him the freedom of a chair.

The whole thing was so simple that, in my conceit, I began to think that I was a bit of a genius insofar as cats were concerned. A little modesty and I would have given more credit to Uncle Timothy, who was really becoming very quick in the uptake. I always warmly congratulated him on his performances and he always purred away with delight. One minor complication arose when both armchairs were vacant but it was considered, for one reason or another, that only one was available to the cat. 'Hup! Hup!' soon got him into an armchair without delay but he made his own choice of which one it was to be. If he chose wrongly from your point of view it was easy to transfer him to the other one. He did not object to this, settling down happily in what was his second choice, but it rather took the polish off the exercise. However, it was easy to solve this problem. I found that I only had to invite him with my 'Hup! Hup!' and point an arm towards the chair which was at his disposal and he would go to that one rather than the other. It is true that we had one or two *contretemps* in the early stages, when he ignored the pointing finger and nipped into the chair he wanted the most. On these occasions, however, I put him back on the hearthrug with a growling rebuke and, at least for half-an-hour, did not invite him to get in any chair at all. The lesson sunk in and he soon ceased to take liberties. Admittedly, even today a mood of sheer impishness gets hold of him on rare occasions. He seems to pretend that he is so short-sighted that he cannot clearly see in which direction my arm is pointing. So he leaps up into the wrong chair. He repents it on the floor.

This treatment for wrong behaviour may sound harsh to some of my readers. Remember, however, that once a lesson is learnt what I suppose might be construed as a punishment is seldom necessary. More important is the fact that if an order is given to an animal, if the creature does the wrong thing and is allowed to get away with it, confusion arises in his own mind.

Uncle Timothy could now appreciate what he was required to do in response to the words 'Out!', 'No!' and 'Hup! Hup!'. They were all useful and, especially having regard to the fact that I had spent relatively little time in his company, I reckoned his performance did him credit. It was, after all, less than five months since we had met. I was really beginning to enjoy the company of Uncle Timothy. In many ways, I had a pretty good idea that this feeling was mutual. It was sad to reflect, when I left Crossgill after that Easter, that I might be lucky if we met up on a dozen days over the next four months. Until the end of the summer I would be unable to do any more to further his education. I had, however, ample time to plan my next move. I adjured his landlady not to be too soft-hearted and to maintain the discipline that I had instilled into the cat. I had not appreciated that, at least to some extent, Uncle Timothy was at heart a one-man cat.

As for me, I adored the brute – and at that time I had not even got a photograph to remind me of him!

V

It would be romantic to describe the summer of 1974, insofar as myself and Uncle Timothy were concerned, as the summer of our discontent. It is true that we saw little of each other but all the evidence showed that Uncle Timothy was very contented indeed. As far as the weather was concerned it was a poor season, generally rather chilly, with a fair amount of rain and comparatively little sun. But for a hunting cat, living in a quiet, pastoral district that nourished a fair supply of rabbits, all free of the ghastly scourge of myxomatosis, it was probably very good indeed. I sometimes thought of Uncle Timothy during those months, but I am fairly certain that he never thought of me.

Whether a cat ever remembers a person in his or her absence is a question which I suppose nobody could answer with any certainty. Maybe a town cat pent up for long periods in restricted quarters, sleeping much of the time away in sheer boredom, might have more time to attempt the exercise; but the life of a healthy, rural cat is far too full of happenings to give it much time for reflection. Where two cats have been living together under the same roof for some time, if death takes one of them, my experience is that the survivor appears to 'miss' his old buddy, frequently prowling around as if seeking him, at least for the first few days.

I believe, however, that relatively intelligent animals – cats and dogs, for example – can 'remember back' in that many of them can instantly recognise, even after a considerable interval of time, an old and familiar 'friend'. For the sake of the cat I had been compelled to part with old Uncle Whiskers after we had enjoyed seven years together. I kept in touch but there were times when many weeks elapsed between one visit and the next. Yet I only had to call him by name and then, even if he could not see me, he responded at once by plodding in my direction.

Cats, generally speaking, strike me as being philosophical creatures. This may be just as well, bearing in mind the casual, offhand sort of way in which many of them are treated. They make the most of what life has to offer and during that summer of 1974, when I was only with Uncle Timothy for brief periods, I had no doubt that he was enjoying a very full life. Actually he was just beginning to show that he was a rabbit-hunting cat of the first class. I shall describe this later but as it involved hours of reconnoitring and long spells of patient stalking, even the long days of summer left him with no time for boredom. There was little reason to suppose that he missed my company but it was pleasant to discover, when I plodded up the fellside from the inn, that he could recognise my voice. I used to call him up and if he was within earshot he would come eagerly, often suddenly appearing on a drystone wall and running the length of it to reach me. His ability to move at good speed along the uneven top of a stone dyke was almost uncanny. But there was no doubt that he instantly recognised an old friend, even by voice alone, after a longish absence.

When Uncle Timothy had first come in from the cold he almost certainly continued to visit the village for a few days. During the preceding weeks, when he had been occupying his rough and ready sleeping-quarters in the old barn loft he had probably foraged in the village during the hours of darkness. He must have been hard-pressed, during cold and often snowy days before Christmas, even to assuage the worst pangs of hunger. Rabbits and rats and mice would have been in short supply on the open fellside at that season. He might well have had a better chance of nabbing a rat or a mouse in the village and I have no doubt that he regularly scrounged round the dustbins for any odd scraps, however unsavoury, that might be lying around. When he had first landed up in something approaching a feline paradise, Uncle Timothy, skinny and half-starved, would gobble up a bit of stale, crusty bread as if it were manna from heaven.

One evening, only two or three days after his arrival, I was walking down to the inn at about nine o'clock. Uncle Timothy had been out when I left his landlady. The bridge across the river is at the foot of the loaning and, as I approached, a black and white cat came prancing across the broad parapet on one side of the bridge. I was fairly sure it was Uncle Timothy but I did not call to him because, at that stage, he had not really learnt his own name. He caught sight of me and scurried off down the roadway. The following morning I discovered that Uncle Timothy had arrived on the window-sill, seeking admission for the night, within ten minutes of this incident, which makes it pretty certain that the cat which I saw was indeed his lordship. This, in turn, confirms my belief that he used to revisit his old haunts in the village for at least a few days, perhaps a week or two, after he had found his new home.

With good board and lodging, the necessity to go ascrounging in the village came to an end. By the time spring arrived he was beginning to mark out for himself some sort of a territory. Thus when his landlady went down the loaning each morning to fetch her newspaper and collect various items from the village shop, Uncle Timothy would often accompany her. The last part of the loaning is very steep and the cat would stop about fifty yards short of the end of it, often jumping up on to one or other of the stone dykes that bound the loaning on either side. Unless something distracted his attention, he would sit there waiting until his landlady returned with her shopping a few minutes later. He would then follow her back to the house. Reckoning that his duties had then been fulfilled he would, if the day was a pleasant one, leave her at the door and go off on the prowl.

Whenever I was staying at the Fox and Hounds Uncle Timothy seemed to be aware of the fact that I walked up the fellside for my breakfast around eight o'clock in the morning. As I trudged up the steep slope I often spotted him sitting on the stone wall, looking out for me. The cat was very wary of all strangers (and still is, for that matter, unless they are invited into the house when, in some peculiar feline way, he reckons them to be non-hostile). Yet although I did not call to him he was able to recognise me over a distance of many yards and, jumping off the wall, he would come trotting down to greet me. After receiving an appropriate welcome he would follow me up the loaning to the house. This kind of thing was what made him such a companionable animal and there was no question of any 'cupboard-love' entering into it, because he was never given any 'titbits' between meals and the only reward he ever got for good behaviour was a bit of cos-

70

setting. He had already shown something of his intelligence. He was rapidly developing into a topper of a cat. Only Uncle Whiskers, upon whose grave he sat with some regularity, rivalled him among all the many cats I had known.

VI

Uncle Timothy's landlady had feared that once the really long days of summer came her lodger might keep late and irregular hours. I thought myself that this was a distinct possibility because sunset at Crossgill in June and most of July is not until after 9.30 and on fine evenings the twilights linger on until midnight. However, as I have already explained, there was little or no trouble. There was an additional incentive for Uncle Timothy to return home in the evenings when, during the summer of 1974, his landlady bought a packet of a proprietary brand of cat food of a sort that Uncle Whiskers had once enjoyed. It was claimed that this stuff would provide a balanced diet for a cat. The food was in the form of small, hard, nutty granules. Given a small handful of these pellets on a plate, Uncle Timothy made it clear that he considered they were delicious, and he always got a ration of them last thing in the evening.

After seeing little of Uncle Timothy for a full four months, I fetched up again at the Fox and Hounds for the last week in August. In fact I only managed four clear days in the village but it was better than nothing. Uncle Timothy gave me what one might almost describe as an effusive welcome. I listened to all the latest news concerning his welfare and was glad to see that he had developed into a magnificent specimen physically. Apart from building up to something approaching his proper weight, he had certainly grown a little during the back-end of the winter and into early spring. Lying flat, with his black, bushy tail stretched out straight, he only just failed to measure a yard from snout-tip to tail-tip, the actual figure being thirty-four and a half inches. I always refer to him as a 'yard of cat' and the exaggeration, less than five per cent, can scarcely be regarded as gross. In weight he was around fourteen pounds, which is probably a fair weight for his length and breadth, especially as he is very big in the bone and uncommonly broad-chested. He is short-furred but his chest-measurement, with the tape-measure held really tight, is just over eighteen inches.

When I was told about the pellets which the cat was given at the end of the day and which he obviously greatly relished, it immediately occurred to me that something of a ceremony might be made of this. The big cardboard packet was kept in the bottom compartment of a cupboard that stood on the kitchen floor. As these pellets had been referred to as Timothy's 'nuts', it seemed to me that this was the name under which they should be known. Uncle Timothy now reacted to four words: Out, No, Hup-Hup and Come-Come (or Coop-Coop). Nuts would not be easily confused with any of these. The drill for the evening ritual was simple enough.

Instead of having these food pellets presented to him on a plate, he would first have to learn to react in the correct way to the word 'nuts!'. This signal would be given to him in the sitting-room (or, for the matter of that, anywhere else where he might be in the late evening). On the word 'nuts!' he would (so I hoped) accompany to the kitchen cupboard in which they were kept whoever was going to give him this *bon-bouche* of the day. A handful of nuts, perhaps a dozen, would then be shaken out into the palm of the hand, the packet put back and the cupboard door closed. Holding a fistful of pellets, one would then retire to the sitting-room, repeating the word 'nuts!' as often as it might be necessary in order to get the cat to follow. Sitting in a chair, holding the pellets in the fist of the right-hand, Uncle Timothy would be invited to jump on one's lap with an invitatory 'Hup! Hup!', when the savoury pellets would be fed to him, one or two at a time, from the half-open palm of the left-hand.

It was not a complicated ritual and, with the cat as keen as mustard to get at the pellets, there was no reason to suppose that it would be very difficult to get him to carry it out perfectly. However, one has to start off from scratch, because the animal has not got the slightest notion of what you have in your mind. Patience is the keyword.

I was able to take him through the first four nightly exercises of the 'nuts' drill. On the first night he was resting on the hearthrug, probably waiting for a call to the kitchen to receive his beloved pellets on a plate. He had been regularly enjoying this nightly treat for a month and more. I called him by name, to attract his attention. But when I said 'Nuts' I was not in the least surprised that he looked at me in utter bewilderment. He may even have thought that 'nuts' was what I was! I got up and walked slowly to the kitchen, repeating 'Nuts! nuts!' as I went. I did not expect the cat to follow me, which was just as well. Although he was alert and watching me, he remained on the hearthrug.

However, standing by the cupboard that contained the precious packet of pellets, I called 'Coop! coop! Tim' reckoning rightly that he would respond to this familiar call. He was already astonishingly biddable and now, glory be, I got an unexpected bonus. He knew quite well where the nuts were kept and this being the time of day when he had learnt to expect his regular ration, he rubbed his head against the corner of the cupboard, purring loudly in anticipation. I deliberately kept him waiting for about half-a-minute, repeating the word 'nuts' in the hope that it would sink in. Then I got out the packet, poured a few pellets into my right hand and replaced it. I closed my fist on the pellets. Uncle Timothy watched my hand, wide-eyed, well aware that the delicacies were held in it. Again I kept on repeating the word 'Nuts'. Uncle Timothy gave me a somewhat baffled, 'What! no plate' sort of look. He was certainly nonplussed when I retreated to the sitting-room but he followed obediently when I called him. I settled into an armchair. The cat sat down at my feet, still puzzled, but eagerly gazing up at me with his green eyes. I kept on saying 'nuts' for a few seconds. Then I gave him the 'Hup Hup!' and he sprang easily and gently on to my knee. Laps were no longer big enough adequately to accommodate his bulk, so he stood up, purring loudly. He was intelligent enough to know that the longed-for pellets were hidden in the fist of my right hand, because he biffed his big head up against it repeatedly. 'Nuts! nuts!' I cried and he sang all the louder. If I uttered the word once I must have uttered it fifty times or more. I spilled the pellets, one by one, into the palm of my other hand and as he dug his head in to gobble up each pellet in turn I went on saying 'Nuts!'.

The following night I did not have to call him to the kitchen. I cried 'Nuts!' and he preceded me to the cupboard. If he hardly put a foot wrong on this second performance, he knew the drill to perfection at the third attempt. Admittedly the procedure was fairly straightforward but I still reckoned the cat was pretty clever to master it so swiftly and faultlessly.

The ceremony of the 'nuts' has been a nightly ritual ever since. When Uncle Timothy's landlady has guests staying in the house it is something of a star turn, and there is competition to be allowed to play the leading part in the ceremony. As Uncle Timothy does not mind who officiates so long as he gets the tasty pellets, he is always ready to play his part to perfection. His is, after all, the leading part and he usually manages to bring the house down. Encores, however, are strictly forbidden. It is a once-nightly show and nowadays, as soon as it is completed, Uncle Timothy bows out gracefully to his admirers and takes himself up to bed. If this is, perhaps, the showiest of all his learnt performances, the tuition involved was minimal, which is more than I can say for some of the other lessons I have taught him. The most difficult exercise of them all, perhaps for the scholar but certainly for the teacher, was still to come. At that time, had I been making out a school report for Uncle Timothy, I would have summed him up: 'An apt pupil, eager to learn. Manners impeccable'.

VII

After seeing very little of him during the summer of 1974, I had rather better opportunities to get to know Uncle Timothy in the following autumn and winter. There was still one instruction that I wanted him to master but as I reckoned that it would require both patience and time and as it was also an exercise that could hardly be really launched, let alone perfected, in the course of even a long week-end it was prudent to postpone it. It would be ideal, I felt, to leave it until the New Year when, as usual, I planned to be in Crossgill for a week or ten days.

It was pleasant enough, through the fall, simply to enjoy the company of Uncle Timothy whenever I could. He had developed into a most companionable creature – a happy characteristic which might be partly attributed to his amiable, easy-going nature but was mostly due to the fact that he had become such a biddable creature. Without this training he might have been much like the average cat and the average cat can scarcely be dubbed 'companionable'. It almost hurts me, these days, to watch some friend call his cat and to see the beast amble off in the opposite direction. The man is probably so accustomed to his cat giving him the brush off that he does not mind but, in the light of my adventures with Uncle Timothy, he looks more than a bit of a fool. Any cat, unless it is grossly neglected, costs quite a lot of money over the course of a year.

Maybe I am selfish but I expect a reasonable return for the expenditure of hard-earned cash. I do not enjoy being treated like a doormat, either by a dog or cat.

In the fall of 1974 I tried taking Uncle Timothy for a few more walks. Somehow my heart was not in the exercise and although the cat would do most of the things I asked of him, such as coming up to my call if he lagged behind or stopping to a 'No!' if he got too far ahead, I had a shrewd suspicion that his heart was not in these walks either. It crossed my mind yet again that it might be far better if the cat took me for a walk, although the notion seemed a little absurd. However, the following year I did (with the surprisingly willing help of the cat) put this idea into practice with considerable success.

It was rewarding enough, that autumn, to spend a good deal of time in the company of Uncle Timothy. All my patient instruction made the cat so much more entertaining than he would otherwise have been, quite apart from the fact that he was never an undisciplined nuisance in the house. In my long absences his landlady kept up the good work but I confess my male *ego* received a bit of a boost when it was reported to me that he was never quite so biddable to her as he was to me.

Cats and humans live very largely in different worlds. I am as incapable of stalking a rat or a rabbit and killing it with my bare hands as Uncle Timothy is of reading a book. In order to strike up a mutual friendship with an animal it is necessary to exploit the common ground. When Uncle Timothy is out hunting it would nullify his chances of success if I tagged along too, although I have once witnessed a patient stalk which ended successfully. But any time spent in the company of the cat – and all my experience leads me to believe that it would be impossible to take on more than one cat at a time – both out of doors as well as in the house, will yield a rich and sometimes unexpected dividend.

It had never been my intention, when teaching Uncle Timothy to obey a few simple instructions, to turn him into a sort of performing animal. I dislike mere parlour-tricks. A Scottie standing up on its hind legs and begging for food at the table apparently gives some people a lot of pleasure and it is none of my business to interfere with the pleasures of others, but to my jaundiced eye the dog looks ridiculous. He would probably get the titbits, anyway, without any un-canine pirouetting. I dislike seeing a bunch of elephants being made to stand up on their hind-legs at a circus, not because I think the elephants object or that any cruelty is necessarily involved in their training but because it strikes me as more than mildly degrading to see one of the noblest of God's creatures behaving in this way. Worse still, the guffaws of the audience seem to me to rob grown men and women (I readily forgive the children) of their own dignity. For these reasons the training I had in mind was intended only for the useful purpose of making the cat's life in a human household more agreeable to the humans and to him.

Throughout his first year's schooling, I became increasingly aware that there was one important omission in Uncle Timothy's education. If a reasonably well-trained dog is making a nuisance of himself, with one sharp order he can be dispatched to his basket. Cats, as well as dogs, are capable of making a nuisance of themselves from time to time. For instance, if food is being prepared in the kitchen cats will usually get wind of it. They will bother about and get under one's feet

81

and even attempt to get on the table on which the culinary preparations are taking place. If, on such an occasion, Uncle Timothy, with his exceptional 'nose' for good food, became obstreperous, he could at least be partly controlled with a sharp negative. But he would still remain in the kitchen. Again, on those comparatively rare occasions when he wanted to go out without good reason later in the evening than was permissible, he would make to jump up on the sitting-room table. A sharp 'No!' would certainly stop him in his tracks but he would probably go into the kitchen and mew softly at the backdoor. This behaviour could be ignored to some extent, but it was still distracting, especially as he would probably pad back into the sitting-room, obviously intent on leaping up on to the table again, and once again had to be stopped with a negative. This behaviour would not continue for very long, because he soon appreciated that he was wasting his time, but it was irritating enough whilst it did last.

I considered, correctly as things turned out, that to teach Uncle Timothy to go and either sit or lie on a certain object on being given a specific word of command might well be fraught with difficulties. Even if I knew him well enough to believe that it could be done, I was loathe to invest five pounds in purchasing a basket of a size sufficient to contain his bulk. At the very end of 1974, when I first arrived at the Fox and Hounds in Crossgill almost on the eve of the New Year festivities, I discussed my ideas with Uncle Timothy's landlady. She agreed that she would be the chief beneficiary if I ever succeeded in putting theory into practice but I sensed that she was even more dubious than I was of bringing this operation to a satisfactory conclusion. Helpfully, however, she suggested one of the means towards attaining the end, which was better than nothing. She produced an upholstered, rubber-foam filled cushion that was one of a set of three which had once fitted into a settee. The cushion was somewhat on the small side, being only about two feet long and a foot wide, and the upper surface sloped at an angle of some ten degrees, but this would have to do.

'Sit!' was to be the magic word that would send Uncle Timothy scurrying to the cushion, which I placed in the sitting-room beside the hearthrug. I gave the cat a day to get accustomed to it but he did not seem to think much of it. Apart from a sniff or two, with which almost any cat will greet an alien object, he ignored it. He continued to hug the hearthrug or, if invited, to lie in an armchair.

My first step was to associate 'Sit!' with the cushion. There could be no question of any long-range stuff at the outset. I chose a moment when he was sitting, washing himself after a meal, on the hearthrug. 'Sit! Sit!' I said, patting the cushion, which was not much more than a cat's paw away from him. Uncle Timothy, bless him, was polite enough to stop washing. He gazed at me, then at my hand patting the cushion, then back at me. It all made no sort of sense to him. So, repeating the word 'Sit!' as I did so, I picked him up by the scruff and placed him on the cushion. When he immediately moved to get off it, I stopped him easily with a sharp 'No!' He sat on the cushion, not altogether comfortably because of the slope, until he decided he might as well lie down. He soon fell asleep, with his hind legs sprawled off on the hearthrug.

If this was a start, progress was slow. Uncle Timothy, naturally enough, was unable to see much point in the cushion. He already had the hearthrug or, if allowed, the chair. He appeared to rate the cushion no better than the rug, both being inferior to an arm-chair. It might well have been simpler to get the cat to associate the command 'Sit!' with the hearthrug but this would have led to all sorts of difficulties. Uncle Timothy was a hardy cat and in warmer weather I knew he would not wish to sit in front of a fire. It was also envisaged that he would be asked to 'Sit!' in other rooms. So the cushion it had to be, however slow progress might be. And it was slow, not least because, in training of this kind, one cannot forcibly remove the cat once he has obediently settled. Several hours may elapse between one single bit of practice and the next. I did not expect much real progress in the week at my disposal, nor did I get it. I just about got the cat to the stage at which the word 'Sit!' was associated in his mind with the cushion. If I was present when he strolled into the room, my word of command influenced him, somewhat reluctantly, to take the cushion instead of the hearthrug. But if he was already sitting on the rug, he would not shift to the cushion; then, as it would be fatal to let the order 'Sit!' go by default, I had to take him by the scruff and place him on it. My impression was that these opening moves were not only unproductive but about as boring for the cat as for myself. But hope springs eternal! I impressed upon Uncle Timothy's guardian the necessity to keep the cat in practice, leaving it to my next visit to take the exercise further.

If I could have been with Uncle Timothy for a month without a break progress would have been much quicker. With long intervals between visits, many of which were merely week-ends, it was much slower than I had hoped, although it became more interesting and rewarding as the exercise was perfected. Once the cat had really got it fixed in his noddle that 'Sit' meant 'cushion', it was time to start on the long-range work. Sometimes driven to the limit of my patience by the slow progress of the earlier stages, this was not only good fun but went better than I expected. By Easter of 1975 it was possible to say 'Sit!' when the cat was in the kitchen and he would at once walk, sedately and with proper regard to his own dignity, to the cushion. It was comical to notice how, on his way to the cushion, he would glance momentarily at a vacant arm-chair but, by this time, he rarely succumbed to the temptation.

The other large front room in the house is a music-room complete with a fine hi-fi stereo reproducer, for Uncle Timothy's landlady is devoted to music as well as to cats. In the winter months a fire was often lit in this room and the cushion was transferred there. This caused a certain amount of confusion for the cat. There was one occasion when the cushion had been left in the music-room from the previous day. I had arrived in Crossgill and, knowing nothing of this, had gone up to visit the cat and found he was being bothersome in the kitchen. 'Sit! Sit!' I shouted. Uncle Timothy at once obediently set course for the sitting-room but, halfway across the room, he suddenly realised that there was no cushion there. He was completely baffled as to what to do, finally looking round at me and giving a plaintive mew of utter bewilderment. After that a second cushion was brought into use, so that there was one in each room.

Once this stage was reached there was little further trouble. Even if one was in the sitting-room and the cat was in the hall or the kitchen, he would come to the cushion when given the appropriate order. There was seldom or never any reason to chase him up from the rear, enforcing the order to sit with a mild stamp of the foot, as had happened in the earlier stages. Even if Uncle Timothy was either upstairs or sitting just outside the house, the word 'Sit!' had the desired result. All this made six months of hard labour more than worthwhile. It must be admitted, however, that once in a while Uncle Timothy got the devil in him and took the bit between his teeth. At these times, when told to sit, he would race out of the kitchen (always a bad sign!) and, instead of entering the sitting-room he would scamper away upstairs. Occasionally he got the better of his landlady in these encounters simply by exhausting her physically. There is no doubt that he rather enjoyed these 'games' but he never got the better of me when I was present. I hunted him down no matter how long it took and, yelling 'No! No! *No*!' in his ear I carried him down to the cushion by the scruff. He was well aware that he was temporarily very much out of favour – and he did not like it at all.

VIII

During the summer of 1975 Uncle Timothy showed his skills in stalking and catching rabbits. He always carried these rabbits back to the garden to eat them but, unfortunately, his landlady did not keep a record of them. Most of his rabbits were young ones, not more than a month or two old. Myxomatosis was rare in this remote district but rabbits are by no means plentiful and Uncle Timothy must be one of the best rabbit-clearance societies the world has ever known. His rabbiting season lasted from March until October. He must have accounted for around seventy in 1975 and this is supported by his tally for 1976, about which I shall write shortly. In the meantime it is important to explain how I came to discover the extent of his territory.

My attempts to take Uncle Timothy for walks, as I have said, were rather unsuccessful, half-hearted affairs. So one fine day, when he was sitting on the stone wall at the back of the house and was evidently about to go off on a foray, I decided to follow him. I trailed along behind him for most of the time, stopping respectfully whenever he stopped to investigate a drain, a patch of rough ground, some ruined building, a rabbit burrow or any other matter that required his attention.

Once started, these companionable walks became a regular feature. If the cat was sitting on the wall outside the house he soon understood that if I said 'walks' with some enthusiasm I was ready to follow him wherever he chose to take me. He was seldom ready to start at once. He would look this way and that, as if weighing up in his own mind which route was likely to be the most profitable from his point of view. He had three or four main routes to and from the house, with several minor variations. Many of these walks of his were in the nature of rabbiting 'recces', and gave me a clear idea of what he considered to be his territory. It was generally longer than it was wide, extending up to a ruined farm about a hundred feet above and rather more than a quarter of a mile to the north-west of his home and eastward to another ruined farm about one third of a mile away. In a straight line it was not much more than half a mile from one of these old farmhouses to the other, whilst the width of his territory varied between two hundred and four hundred yards.

It is often said that a 'doctored' Tom loses his spunk. This has not been my experience, although I have no doubt that individual Toms vary, whether castrated or not. Uncle Whiskers, for all his lack of armour after his accident, drove off any strange cat and stood his ground with any dog. Uncle Timothy is made in the same mould, except that he often succeeds in chasing dogs away. He enjoys periodic encounters with a terrier and he has more than once seen a noisy mongrel, probably twice his own weight, off the premises. His technique with dogs is simple and effective. If he is on a stone dyke when one comes within his orbit he makes a point of getting down to its level. He does not pick a quarrel but watches the dog like a lynx. If it approaches he sits facing it, tail down but with one paw slightly raised off the ground, ready to strike. He does not raise the fur along his back, as cats are apt to do if they are frightened. I doubt if he is frightened. Dog and cat stare at one another a few feet apart. The dog may or may not bark but Uncle Timothy keeps up a continuous low growl, never once taking his eyes off his opponent. The dog does not like this and, sooner or later, slowly turns to slink away. Then the cat usually springs after him and the dog beats a hasty retreat. In the case of the terrier the cat runs him pretty close until he has crossed the edge of his territory. However, my guess is that Uncle Timothy would prefer a world without dogs. One trespassing dog can utterly ruin a hunting day!

Uncle Timothy, like almost all good hunting cats, always brings his trophies back to the garden. They are usually still alive when he returns with them. Although he does not 'play' with them and is, in fact, very anxious to eat them, they seldom die quickly unless one intervenes. Unfortunately, from the outset, he fiercely resented any interference whatsoever. If one approached he would growl and then move quickly off with the bunny held firmly in his strong jaws, causing it to squeal in a heart-rending way, although I am not convinced that the cries are evidence of either pain or terror. Nevertheless, it is the responsibility of any person to curtail any unnecessary suffering by any creature that may have fallen victim to their cat, be it rabbit, rat or bird. In the case of Uncle Timothy this was more easily said than done. I very soon appreciated that, if one went on chasing him from pillar to post, the suffering of the rabbit, far from being curtailed, was likely to be considerably prolonged. So I changed my technique.

I approached him very slowly, calling him by name in my most congratulatory tone of voice. The congratulations were always deserved, anyway, because catching a rabbit in open country calls for considerable skill and endless patience on the part of a cat. He used to swear at me like a trooper in my earlier efforts to get the rabbit from him. He would often carry it ten or fifteen yards before settling down again, still growling. I pursued him, still walking slowly and giving him the 'good-boyo' stuff. He might shift a third or even a fourth time but, eventually, he allowed me to catch up with him. I then stooped down, choosing my moment to get hold of him by the scruff of the neck and then, holding him up, I prized the bunny from his jaws, killed it and immediately returned it to him. Apart from the fact that it was his rabbit, not mine, I knew that he would never have trusted me again if I had not given it back to him.

I handled several rabbits in this way. He gradually got accustomed to this drill, until eventually he stopped moving away and seldom growled. Nowadays I can get a rabbit away from him within half a minute (this being occupied in the quiet approach and the honeyed words). I no longer have to seize him by the scruff. He relinquishes the bunny without a murmur. He knows well enough, now, that it will be returned at once and it certainly makes no difference to him whether it is alive or dead. He eats it, as all cats do, from the head downwards. But unlike any cat I have ever known he eats almost the whole lot, flesh, skin and bones. To listen to him cracking and champing the bigger bones makes it easy to appreciate why he came in from the cold with one half-broken tooth. How he digests the skin and fur I do not know, but he has never been sick or even indisposed after swallowing an entire rabbit except the guts, the ends of the hind legs and the scut. He can demolish a small bunny, of three quarters of a pound, in five or ten minutes. But when he walks away, anybody viewing him from behind might be excused for thinking that he was a pregnant Quean – and one pretty far gone in her pregnancy, too!

During this fine summer of 1976, whilst I have been writing this book, I have asked Uncle Timothy's landlady to keep an exact record of the number of rabbits caught by the cat. He caught his first one on March 17 and got another five during the next six days, including two in one day. All these were very small and he probably relieved the doe rabbit of her whole family. He caught no more in March, so far as was known, and only five in April. However, by the end of May his tally had risen to 23, to which total he added another 15 in June. Now, at the end of August, he is just about to exceed the tally of 35 brace, which figure I felt was a likely target for the year and as this crop has all been culled off an area of less than 150 acres he is not only a good ally of the farmer but also a fine guard-cat for the one or two householders within the area who have vegetable gardens.

Small fry simply do not interest him. Whereas ginger Sam catches scores of field-mice and shrews in the course of a summer, Uncle Timothy catches next to none. He is no longer interested in birds, either, but he is a nailer on any rat that dares to show its head, although he never attempts to eat them. He did once kill a bird and a rat on the same day, however. The bird really committed suicide. Uncle Timothy was sitting peacefully on a drystone wall sunning himself on a balmy autumn afternoon when a tiny wren kept prancing about on the top of the wall, popping in and out of the holes and cracks, clicking away until, at long last, he roused the interest of the cat. With one spring the cat got rid of this noisy nuisance and flung it aside. An hour or so later he killed a rat in the barn.

July 11, 1976, was something of a red-letter day for me. Most of Uncle Timothy's rabbits have been caught in my absence. Apart from that, it might interfere with his chances of success always to follow him when he is hunting. On this particular morning, however, both Uncle Timothy and ginger Sam were sitting on a dry-stone wall overlooking a large area of nettles. I strolled over and joined them, looking over the wall but keeping still, happy in the knowledge that we were all three downwind of the nettles, in which I was sure a young bunny was on the move because I had been told that Uncle Timothy had been watching that patch, off and on, for the previous three days.

I could see nothing but both cats could see or hear something. Except as an onlooker, however, Sam took no active part in what followed. After some minutes Uncle Timothy scampered briskly past my nose, running along the top of the wall, rather over four feet in height, until he was directly above the far end of the nettle-patch. He crouched on the wall, tensed up with excitement. I got the impression that at any moment his eyes might pop out of his head. Suddenly he slid smoothly over the edge of the wall, then quickly checked himself and remained as still as a statue. He was now in a position which I would have considered it impossible for any cat to maintain for more than a few seconds. It is true that he just had his hind paws on the edge of the top of the wall but his full weight was on his front ones, one of which was a foot in front of the other and little more than two feet from the ground. By all the laws of gravitation it was surely an impossible position for any cat to maintain but maintain it he did, without a flicker of a movement, for at least a minute. Then the rabbit must have moved. He was on it in a flash. There was a scream and Uncle Timothy jumped up from beyond the nettles on to the top of the wall with the bunny in his mouth. When I took it from him it weighed, I reckoned, just about a pound, which was above his average. Unlike Uncle Whiskers, he does not catch full-grown rabbits – perhaps he is just a wise enough guy not to kill the goose that lays the golden eggs!

IX

Unlike the summer of 1974, which was generally rather wet and chilly, that of 1975 was notably sunny and warm. Most cats, like most humans, prefer genial weather although, with their fur coats, they appear more or less immune to all but the severest of frosts. Whilst a shower or even a steady drizzle of rain may be ignored, few cats care to get really wet. But what they loathe, in my experience, is a very strong or gale-force wind. It follows that cats spend more time indoors in winter than in summer and more time outside in a fine summer than in a stormy one.

It was not until the fine summer of 1975 that something like a friendship developed between Uncle Timothy and ginger Sam. The ginger cat was rising ten years when one-year-old Timothy came on the scene. Furthermore, by that time Sam had had the establishment all to himself throughout the fifteen months that had elapsed since the death of Uncle Whiskers. Left to himself, he had become rather lazy. In the idleness of a long winter he had put on weight which, in its turn, tended to make him lazier than ever. Uncle Timothy's advent rattled him into some periods of winter activity which was physically good for him, but for a long time Sam made it clear that he had no great liking for the newcomer. This period of the cold war, for which the ginger was entirely responsible, might not have been so prolonged if his new 'companion' had been less amiable in his disposition. I have known several benevolent cats but Uncle Timothy is alone in being utterly devoid of any sort of malice. In almost three years he has never once attempted to scratch or bite anybody, in spite of being subjected to some strict discipline. Looking back on my debut as a cat-trainer it never ceases to astonish me that when I was thwarting his wishes, he not only never had a slash at me with an open-clawed paw but that I never once feared that he might do so. Physically a very strong cat and a mighty hunter of rabbits, Uncle Timothy is the gentlest animal which it has ever been my privilege to handle.

I suspect it was this amiable disposition that prevented the younger and stronger cat from retaliating when ginger Sam responded to his friendly approaches with a slash of his paw. This ill-mannered and somewhat cantankerous behaviour on the part of Sam went on, if with decreasing intensity, for more than a year. It was that fine summer of 1975 that changed the situation quite dramatically in a matter of weeks, yet this was eighteen months after the arrival of Uncle Timothy within the orbit of ginger Sam!

It all began with ginger Sam deciding to follow Uncle Timothy on his forays. They would stroll off together like a couple of buddies, ginger Sam usually a few yards behind his black and white partner. Uncle Timothy would sit on some vantage point, such as the top of a stone wall, which gave him a wide view of part of his hunting territory. He might already know that there were young rabbits about in the vicinity but more often than not he would be engaged in the patient reconnaissance so essential to ultimate success. Ginger Sam would sit fairly close to him, lacking the concentration of the younger cat and becoming more and more bored.

If Uncle Timothy sensed that there were rabbits about he would sit watchfully for several hours. On these occasions ginger Sam, suffering from ennui, would come home on his own. On the other hand if, within the hour, Uncle Timothy saw nothing to raise his hopes he might well decide to return home before ginger Sam got fed up with the proceedings, in which case the two cats would stroll home together. The cold war was over.

The effect on ginger Sam was dramatic. He not only revelled in this new companionship but, because he started to take much more exercise, began to lose weight. Overweight cats, like overweight dogs and humans, are unhealthy. Now well into his twelfth year, ginger Sam is scarcely recognisable as the cat that he was two years ago. He does not carry an ounce of superfluous flesh, is fit and active and can leap up to the top of a five-foot drystone wall with comparative ease.

In losing weight ginger Sam has also lost his cantankerous streak. During the summer of 1975 the two cats started taking their afternoon siesta together in the summerhouse. However, ginger Sam was unwilling to shed all his reserve at once. They slept on old coats on separate, if adjacent, table-tops. Ginger Sam usually occupied the more spacious bed of the two but Uncle Timothy, amiable as ever, never grumbled about his second-class berth. Within a year, however, they both shared the same bunk, sleeping back-to-back, as happy and contented as a couple of sandboys.

X

By the end of that summer of 1975, especially after I had had a full ten days with him at the end of August, I knew that Uncle Timothy's schooldays were pretty well over. His reactions to the words 'No'; 'Sit'; 'Hup-hup'; 'Nuts' and 'Out' were perfect. He never confused one word with another. 'Nuts', of course, was simply the signal for the start of a nice little ritual ceremony which the cat enjoyed as much as the onlookers.

Apart from 'hup! hup!', a command which, except in the case of the ritual of the nuts, means that he can doss down in one of his favourite armchairs, the cat does not relish taking the orders from strangers, but he will do so if they have enough character to enforce them. He treats his devoted landlady, as he should do, with proper respect in these matters. Very occasionally, usually when he has had a quiet day because of very stormy weather and is, in consequence, brimful of energy even late in the day, the imp gets into him and, on being ordered to 'sit!', he will rush out of the kitchen and gallop off upstairs. Probably he thinks of it in terms of a frolic and sometimes his landlady is too tired to pursue the cat upstairs and enforce the discipline. In earlier days he used to try this on with me and occasionally still does so, now and then, but I always get him down, usually simply by repeatedly calling him to 'sit'. He is, if only by a whisker or two, a 'one-man' cat. He will almost always obey me, quickly and

99

promptly. Maybe this is because I have taught him everything he knows by way of discipline. It was a long and patient business for both of us and, in a way, it led to a pretty close understanding between us.

In the October of 1975, towards the end of the month when I happened to be spending a few days in Crossgill, Uncle Timothy's hospitable landlady arranged a small dinner-party to which I was invited. The other guests were two mutual friends, Charles and Kay Wearmouth. I reckon Charles one of the best and we have a mutual bond in both having flown in the Royal Air Force during the Second World War. Charles, awarded the DFC, was a 'Pathfinder' pilot in Bomber Command. I was a navigator in Coastal Command. Our respective war-time jobs give us both plenty of scope for that sort of chaff which is, understandably, lost on the younger generation. Thus Charles alleges that all navigators invariably got hopelessly lost, which invites my reply that pilots were no better than aerial bus-drivers, depending on their navigators to tell them in which direction they should drive the 'crate'.

I looked forward to that dinner-party – and not only because I knew that I would enjoy good food and wine in excellent company. There was a fifth member of the party who, with any luck, might play a notable part. I made up my mind that this was an opportunity to test the measure of Uncle Timothy's behaviour in public. With any luck I should be able to put him through all his paces and I was determined that the performance was going to be a perfect one. I had enough faith in the cat to feel certain that he would give me all that I was going to ask of him. But I wished him to do things promptly, not with any grudging slowness arising from the presence of strangers. And I did not want him suddenly to take a fancy to an armchair and so have to be checked with a sharp 'No!' when he knew full well that only 'Hup! Hup!' gave him licence to occupy a seat.

About half-past seven on a dry but overcast night the four of us were sipping sherry in the music-room. Uncle Timothy was out and, as the lights in the sitting-room were off I kept a wary eye on the window. There were two geranium plants, so I had to peer closely between the sweet-smelling green leaves. When we went in to dine an hour later the cat had still not appeared. I would have wished to have been placed facing the window, a position which would have also given me close proximity to the cushion by the fire on which I intended the cat should sit as soon as he came back. As it was I was sideways-on to the window and as far from the cat's cushion as I could be, though I could see it over the top of the table provided that the guest placed opposite did not sway about too much.

The feast was in its middle course when Uncle Timothy suddenly appeared and sat outside the window. I drew attention to his arrival and allowed one and all to have a good look at him before I moved to let him in. Against a completely dark background his boldly marked pied suiting was shown off to perfection. When I raised the window I said 'Sit!' almost before the cat had got his head inside. I also said a silent prayer. The cat went straight to the cushion and sat on it. I was so pleased that I gave him a chuck under the chin, which set him off in a rattling purr, before resuming my seat. Yet I had reached a stage where I could almost read the mind of that cat. I sensed that he wanted to get out to the kitchen to see if there might be any 'left-overs' by way of food or drink. Nibbling away at a delicious

101

wedge of prime Stilton cheese, I scarcely dared to take my eye off him. Uncle Timothy knew well enough, however, that he was 'under orders' and when he did make a move he did it furtively and in slow-motion. Very slowly he slid one paw off the cushion and on to the carpet. Not wishing to interrupt the general conversation with a loud negative, I gave a short, low, rasping 'Ach!'. The paw was immediately drawn back on to the cushion. The cat looked over at me with appealing green eyes. I shook my head at him. I have an idea that he has learnt that head-shaking is an unfavourable sign. Anyway, he proceeded to lie down on the cushion and, much relieved, I knew that any immediate danger was over.

After the meal we sat and drank coffee and, whilst doing so, all the most comfortable chairs were occupied. This removed one temptation for Uncle Timothy. Later it was decided that we should retire to the other room to enjoy a little music. This gave me my next opportunity to show off my protegé. Once the guests had risen from their chairs I pointed to one of the two armchairs and cried 'Hup! Hup!' I said it more loudly than usual because, by now, the cat was half-asleep but Uncle Timothy rose at once and jumped into the right chair.

I was rather sorry that I had not had a chance to demonstrate how well the cat always reacted to a sharp 'No!' but that chance came within a few minutes. When indoors Uncle Timothy is a companionable cat, always preferring to be with folk, and after a few minutes he came strolling into the music-room, obviously intent on securing the one comfortable, vacant space, between the two people sitting at either end of the settee. This was only permissible if a coverlet was placed in position to prevent his hairs getting on to the upholstery. I stopped the cat with a sharp negative. He sat down and waited whilst I folded the coverlet to the correct size and placed it in position. One 'Hup! Hup!' and he settled down with a great song of contentment.

To finish up the successful evening I took him through the ceremony of the nuts. This was always a winner with strangers and one could guarantee that Uncle Timothy would carry it off without making the slightest error. When, after he had swallowed the last granule, I stroked him as he stood on my lap to indicate that the nightly ritual was at an end, he jumped down and pottered off to bed. It was raining by now, so the Wearmouths drove me back to the Fox and Hounds. I slept well that night. Uncle Timothy probably slept well, too. He certainly deserved to and, in time, I gave him his reward.

I became increasingly aware, when the cat was bidden to 'sit', that the cushion on which he had to settle was neither particularly comfortable nor really suitable either in size or shape. What he needed, I decided, was a good dog-basket. In the summer of 1976 I bought him one. The smallest size into which he could be expected to fit in reasonable comfort was twenty-four inches in diameter. It cost me just short of five pounds but I did not grudge a penny of it. How could I?

There is not much difference between the words 'sit' and 'basket'. When this splendid basket first replaced the cushion, I used to say: 'Sit. Basket'. Cats, like humans, do not take easily to change and for the first day or two Uncle Timothy was suspicious of the basket, slightly uneasy whenever he was in it. This phase soon passed. Within a week he obviously much preferred it to the old cushion. He very soon understood that the command 'basket' had come to replace the old order 'sit'. Everything would have been smooth sailing had it not been for the fact that his pal, ginger Sam, decided that he liked the new basket, too. There was not room in the one wicker basket for the two of them. So a second basket had to be purchased for ginger Sam. But ginger Sam was not my cat. He belongs to my cat's landlady, so she paid for this second basket. I do sometimes wonder how mean I can get!

XI

My story of Uncle Whiskers ended in the death of the cat. This biography of his successor ends on a happier note. Approaching his fourth birthday Uncle Timothy is in the prime of his life. It seemed to me appropriate to travel north to be with him for a few days whilst writing this final section of the tale of the cat that came in from the cold.

Twice in one day Uncle Timothy walked me for half a mile to a field high above his home. Watching his questing through rough, dried-out grasses it was obvious that there was a bunny around. Every now and then, although the ground was parched and dry, he caught a stale scent and nosed his way for three or four yards before losing it. Under the blazing sun of that August morning I guessed the rabbit was safe in a hole or some other cover. There was no doubt, however, that the cat was satisfied of its presence and I was not surprised when he went up to the same place in the afternoon. I found it too hot to follow him but after the cat had had his supper I went up with him again in the cool of the evening. Anxious not to spoil his chances, I stood and watched from behind a stone wall.

Uncle Timothy laid low in the thick grasses, scarcely visible for long periods. He changed his position, moving slowly, three or four times. I kept an eye open for the bunny but saw nothing. After nine o'clock the twilight began to deepen but the cat, who had been sitting out for over an hour, remained as patient as ever.

The next morning, when I arrived up at the house I was not surprised to learn that Uncle Timothy, on being let out at five o'clock, had made off up-fell towards the same pasture. He had come back for his breakfast and gone off again. I set off and found him in much the same place in the same field. I reckoned that the cat had already covered about a mile and a half on this day. Settling myself under the shade of a stone wall I watched for what might happen. In two hours the cat hardly moved and of a bunny there was no sign. Around noon I gave him a call and he trotted over to me and led me back to the house and both our lunches.

I guessed he would go up to the field in the afternoon but I guessed wrongly. It was very warm and he went about one hundred yards to a dried-out beck which ran through a deep gully. He settled himself on a cool stone under the shade of a rowan or mountain-ash. Even the biggest of boulders make poor couches for a human, so I left him sleeping and climbed out beyond the gully, finally settling myself about two hundred yards beyond and out of sight of the cat. Reclining full-length in the grass, I pulled my deerstalker over my face to keep the flies off and soon dozed. I was awakened as my hat was pushed off my face to find a purring Uncle Timothy staring me in the face. He had had no difficulty in finding me and I suppose he must have followed me by scent alone.

He was happy to stroll back with me to tea. Immediately afterwards he set off again and, anxious to see how much ground he covered in a day, I followed. I was not surprised when we landed up in the same high field he had twice visited in the morning. After two hours of comparative inactivity, during which neither of us glimpsed even the scut of a rabbit, the cat was happy, when I called him, to follow me back to the house. He had now covered over three miles during the day and had probably spent more than five hours sitting in that apparently rabbitless field. It struck me that hope springs eternal in the feline breast as well as in the human one.

After he had eaten his supper I watched him plod up the fell once again. I did not bother to follow at once, knowing exactly where he would be. Around sunset I strolled up and joined him, once again keeping behind a drystone dyke in order not to queer his pitch. The cat moved several times in the twilight, once or twice questing the ground. He was engrossed and I did nothing to interrupt him until the gloaming was almost over. I wanted to feed him his 'nuts' but I also wanted to get back to the inn in time to imbibe a mug of well-earned ale before going to bed. I called the cat and, for once, he failed to respond. I walked over to him and he sat up and greeted me but when I made to move away he would not follow. So I picked him up and carried him off under my crooked arm. He grumbled throatily but made no attempt to 'have a go' at me. After covering about a hundred yards I was glad to put my heavy burden down. He at once started to move back towards his hunting field. I stopped him with a brisk 'No.' I said: 'Coop! Tim' and he began to follow me but once again growled his displeasure. It was almost dark and I knew that if I let him go back he might be tempted to stay out late. I also knew that, most likely, his devoted guardian would stay up to greet his return however late it might be. Walking ahead of me, Uncle Timothy grumbled his way to the last gate. I then uttered the magic word: 'Nuts!' His rumbles of displeasure

107

ceased. He scampered on ahead to the back door. I gave him the longed-for pellets, after which he immediately made off upstairs to bed. He had been out for the better part of sixteen or seventeen hours, had covered more than four miles and was probably weary. I was thirsty but I did not make the Fox and Hounds before closing-time – not that it mattered. Being a resident and a citizen of a country which suffers complicated and wholly absurd licensing laws in the field of liquor, I was able to get my pint and remain within the law. I was also able to give some of my chums a pint, too. Because *I* paid for them, this was also within the law!

The next morning Uncle Timothy caught that bunny – one of the tiniest he has ever brought back. After I had killed it (it weighed barely half-a-pound) he eat the lot and slept for most of the day. It was warm, but in the afternoon I made a complete 'recce' of the whole of Uncle Timothy's territory. It seemed rabbit-less until I came to the ruined farm up to the north-west of the house. I went on to a field beyond and immediately put up a good-sized rabbit, which went off at full-speed. I considered this was too big to figure in Uncle Timothy's menu but after tea, when the cat had got over his lethargy, I took him up to the derelict farm. Although he usually took me for walks, he was quite happy, as on this occasion, to follow me provided that he had no other urgent business on hand.

Once in the field where I had earlier spotted the rabbit, Uncle Timothy suddenly came to life. He quested hither and thither, quartering the ground with obvious interest. I left him there and in due time he, too, arrived back for his supper. Almost immediately he set off again for the ruined farm. I wished him luck.

It was a perfect evening, very still and cool after the heat of the day. A few minutes before sunset I felt I might as well walk up to see what the cat was doing but, having covered half the distance, I thought better of it and settled myself very comfortably where a stone stile made a break in a drystone wall. It really was a superb evening, with a red sun sinking slowly into the north-western fells. Every now and then I gave Timothy a brief call. I had no doubt that he was up in the field beyond the ruined farm and so I kept an eye open in that direction but he did not come. The sun set, the last slice suddenly disappearing as if it had been jerked down. The view was superb and the air so still that I could clearly hear the prattle and laughter of children playing on the village green half a mile below me. I gave Uncle Timothy a call about every five minutes but, as the twilight settled, he still did not appear. A big full moon lurched up above the fells opposite the sunset with a face as red as that of a Somerset farmer. The children had gone home to bed and it was very quiet and good to be alive in such a place with the deepening twilight shrouding the familiar landmarks in an air of insubstantiality. I got the feeling that, if time could have been stopped at that moment, then maybe I could have been happy forever.

Time to go. I took one last glance towards the old farm, etched darkly against the lighter northern sky. Something white, and moving too. I squinted through my binoculars. It was Uncle Timothy. I gave the cat one call and, although he was fully two hundred yards away he looked up at once and then, on a second call, he ran towards me as if for his life, never pausing, finally leaping up on to the wall and getting the cosseting that he expected. It was a fit end to a perfect day.

The next morning Uncle Timothy nailed that rabbit. When I broke its neck before giving it back to the cat I was satisfied that it weighed over two pounds. He could only eat half of it – bones and all, in spite of its size – and he was knocked out for the rest of the day.

Any person meeting Uncle Timothy for the first time would probably appreciate that he is a big, powerful and very active cat. What would intrigue them most, I think, would be his obedience. If it is not a unique feline performance – and I have no desire to make extravagant claims in this matter – it is certainly very unusual to watch a cat which, on being ordered to sit, proceeds quietly to a basket in another room. Not only does he understand perfectly well what he is expected to do (or not to do) in response to half-a-dozen different words of command but he will usually do it without any necessity to repeat the order in louder and sterner tones.

If I had been in his company all the time, instead of for irregular and often very short periods, I believe I could have finished his schooling in a matter of a few months, certainly well within a year. As it was it took me over two years and I would not deny, apt pupil though he was, that it involved the tutor in exercising considerable patience as well as the expenditure of a good deal of time.

The reader may pose the question: 'Was it really worth it?'. I believe it was and for more than one reason. If any cat or dog is going to live with you it has got to give as well as take. It took me considerably more than half a lifetime to appreciate cats at all. I have no interest whatsoever in unresponsive cats which are little better than living ornaments (and expensive ornaments at that). Perhaps I am too selfish, but if a cat is going to get something out of me I want to receive something in return. I dislike the sort of cat that, on being called by its owner, proceeds to stalk off in the opposite direction. One great benefit from my teaching of Uncle Timothy has been that he has learnt to keep regular hours, that he does not hog the best chairs and that he never makes a nuisance of himself about the house. But an even greater bonus arising from his patient schooling has been the understanding which has grown up between us. To achieve success, I have had sometimes to be firm but there has been no bullying on my side nor have I ever once resorted to any physical coercion, even of the gentlest kind, other than to pick him up by the scruff and place him quietly in the place (as in the 'sit' exercises) where I wanted him to be. One had to be patient and one had to realise that, at first, the cat had no idea what he was required to do. But when he did begin to learn, when he did the right things and earned my praises he fairly purred with pleasure. It was a two-way association and it has been the basis of a firm and genuine companionship.

My wish, which once seemed so extravagant, to teach a cat to behave along the lines of a well-trained and intelligent dog is really only a small part of this story. It is the understanding that has developed between the cat and myself which has been so rewarding. It really is good fun to be taken for a walk by a cat, apart from the bonus that you quickly learn the background to his hunting activities. There is much more to catching a bunny in open country than mere luck!

It is satisfactory to own a cat that comes to a call. If he is nearby, Uncle Timothy pops up and comes to you with reasonable speed and, sometimes, even races along. If the cat is several hundred yards away he

111

almost invariably comes home within ten of fifteen minutes. He does not expect to be fed or given some special titbit but he has learnt that he will get a cheerful welcome.

This very morning two well-grown lambs had escaped from a pasture and were charging around outside Uncle Timothy's home. The cat, at the time, was out. Uncle Timothy's landlady went down the lane, opened the field gate and then took up position to act as a 'stop' whilst I quietly drove the lambs down towards her. In the middle of this simple but delicate operation Uncle Timothy came charging out of the gate, wheeled round and took up a position sitting beside the feet of his landlady, facing operations. He may not have understood just what it was all about but he made it very clear that the proceedings were much too fascinating to miss.

Earlier in this book I wrote, quite spontaneously, that I had come to adore Uncle Timothy. I have since carefully considered whether or not I ought to allow those words to stand. In order to be able to claim that you adore something you must hold it in respect and affection. My head tells me that the cat has certainly earned my respect. Affection, on the other hand, is an emotion that springs from the heart. It is never easy to control ones emotions. In the case of Uncle Timothy I find it quite impossible.